Human Factor in Free Market Efficiency

Human Factor in Free Market Efficiency

Fermanian School of Business,
Point Loma Nazarene University,
San Diego, CA, USA.

New Century Publications
New Delhi, India

NEW CENTURY PUBLICATIONS
4800/24, Bharat Ram Road,
Ansari Road, Daryaganj,
New Delhi – 110 002 (India)

Tel.: 011-2324 7798, 4358 7398, 6539 6605
Fax: 011-4101 7798
E-mail: indiatax@vsnl.com • info@newcenturypublications.com
www.newcenturypublications.com

Editorial office:
LG–7, Aakarshan Bhawan,
4754-57/23, Ansari Road, Daryaganj,
New Delhi – 110 002

Tel.: 011-4356 0919

Copyright © 2012 by the author

First Published: **2012**

ISBN: **978-81-7708-290-6**

Published by New Century Publications and printed at Salasar Imaging Systems, New Delhi.

Designs: Patch Creative Unit, New Delhi.

PRINTED IN INDIA

Dedication

standing dead
standing dead
great and mighty tree
standing dead
standing dead
something within my soul
sits at the piano
and plays an inaudible melody
that rings and jingles
only in the deepest corner of my soul
only I but none else hear
the proverbs and metaphors you sing
standing dead
in the parlour of Hwange Park
           Senyo Adjibolosoo (June 22, 1999)

It with great delight I dedicate this book to all my MBA as well as undergraduate students—past and present. Your love for economics has been a great inspiration for me. May our combined efforts, continuing interactions, and fascinating dialogues in diverse forms move the discipline of economics closer to its foundational moral principles so that its true relevance to our perennial problems and challenges will shine.

Foreword

As an admirer of Professor Senyo Adjibolosoo, I am constantly amazed at his ability to look at complex problems and provide reasonable solutions. As our world goes through the throes of economic declines and misunderstood recessions and potential depression, the average person on the street bows his head in total impotence. Even the experts can only try old, tired solutions that never seem to solve our financial dilemma.

This book is a primer on the only way that this world can toss off its continual spiralling from feast to famine. If there is any hope for economic stability, it is based on the principles of human factor theory long promoted by Professor Senyo Adjibolosoo.

The book is easily understood by even the novice and I would have no qualms assigning it as a reading requirement in my high school economics classes if I were still working. It is straight forward and clear as it focuses on the significance of lifestyle choices positioned in the principles of honesty, integrity, love, grace, compassion, and forgiveness. Our subscription to and living by the dictates of these principles in terms of how we treat all people equally will enhance our wealth creation process and quality of life. The decision to live by these principles produces the qualities that make for a successful society as well as a stable economy. I strongly recommend this book to anyone who is concerned about the direction the world's economies are going.

Russ Armstead
Retired High School Teacher of Economics and History

About the Book

Existing knowledge about what makes the free market economy system function efficiently is incomplete, though improving continually. Few scholars of economics possess any idea as to what unleashes the factors that fuel free market efficiency, high economic growth, and sustained human-centered development. The lack of this knowledge has led to warped philosophical economic thinking, theorizing, faulty policies, useless plans, irrelevant projects, and bankrupt programmes.

This book presents the theory and empirical evidence on the human factor foundation of free market efficiency. It demonstrates that the sole variable that underscores the degree of effectiveness of the *laissez-faire* economic system is the quality of the human factor.

Author's Profile

Senyo Adjibolosoo is with the Fermanian School of Business, Point Loma Nazarene University, San Diego, CA, USA.

Contents

Contents

Preface

This book presents the theory and empirical evidence on the human factor foundation of free market efficiency. It demonstrates that the sole variable that underscores the degree of effectiveness of the *laissez-faire* economic system is the quality of the human factor. In the past centuries knowledge about what makes the free market economic system function efficiently was a rare commodity everywhere in the Global Village. Few scholars of economics possess any idea as to what unleashes the factors that fuel free market efficiency, ongoing economic growth, and sustained human-cantered development. The lack of this knowledge has led to warped philosophical economic thinking, theorizing, faulty policies, useless plans, irrelevant projects, and bankrupt programs.

This widespread ignorance regarding the primary factor that either propels or militates against free market efficiency and economic progress poses enormous challenges to our ability to attain and sustain continuing economic growth and human-cantered economic development. This high level of ignorance has also exacerbated the diversely complex economic problems and policy failures that prevail in human communities. These challenges create paralyzing waves of fear and hopelessness regarding what most political leaders and orthodox economists view as reflective of tough economic downturns.

The failure to identify and deal with these realities has dire consequences for long-term quality of life, human welfare, and advancement. The kinds of anxiety, restlessness, and frustrations experienced in most countries regarding recessions/depressions underscore the poverty of true knowledge and a deeper understanding as to how recessions and/or depressions happen and how to get out of them. At best global, national, and community leaders appeal to and apply old and stale theoretical economic solutions to new problems created by old thinking and solutions. They seldom possess insights into the true cause of the economic challenges we face. The argument is made in this book that no people can make their economic system work as efficiently as possible without having first honed the positive qualities of the human factor over time. The critical policy recommendation is that market efficiency requires leaders, subordinates, and patriotic citizens who understand that the most important factor that either propels or hinders economic growth and development is the quality of the human factor. To hone the quality of the human factor is to equip the free market agents and forces to pursue, attain, and sustain optimal outcomes of the wealth creation process.

Acknowledgment

One of the greatest things that can happen to a man or woman is to have a friend who can be trusted under all circumstances. Such a friend is always there for you and is more than willing to provide you with any assistance you may need. Indeed, I have found such a friend in my wife, Sabina. I wish to acknowledge her invaluable contributions to my writing of this book. Without her patience and the willingness to make a great deal of sacrifices, the thought about writing this book would not have become a reality. In the same way, I am grateful to Selassie and Selorm for their contributions to the preparation of this book. Their sacrifices are highly acknowledged.

I also owe a heavy debt to my students and colleagues. My graduate as well as undergraduate students have made tremendous contributions toward the writing of this book for their inputs through discussions in and out of the classroom. May their love for economics as an academic discipline be the leaven to move the discipline from its current doldrums of irrelevance.

July 2011   Senyo Adjibolosoo
San Diego, USA

1

Introduction

I woke up this morning to the screaming of sirens from numerous police cruisers, fire trucks, and ambulances. It was about three o'clock in the morning. The sounds were so ear piercing that I could no longer fall asleep. As a result, I dashed to the family room and turned on the television. On the television screen, I perceived that there were several of these service vehicles parked outside an apartment building. While the paramedics were pulling out their stretchers and hurrying toward the building, policemen and women were located at strategic positions with their guns drawn and pointed toward the building and ready to fire on command. Firemen and women were already positioned strategically and poised for action. Yet since there were no signs of a fire yet, these service men and women were either sitting in or walking around their fire truck, probably wondering about what their next set of action steps would be. There were many onlookers who were clothed with the garments of fear and anxiety. Hopelessness was boldly inscribed on their facial expressions.

While all this drama was unfolding, a policeman who had a megaphone in his right hand was calling and yelling at the top of his voice to the suspect, demanding that he came out of the building. This whole drama had started in the infant hours of the day when a distraught woman called 911 and reported that the boyfriend came in drunk and pointed a gun at her. And while she called 911 and was talking to the individual who picked up the call, three gunshots were heard. As the 911 call receiver's heart began to race, she wondered whether the woman was still alive or not. "Mom! Mom!! Mom!!! Are you there?" She asked with great fear and trepidation. In response to her question, she heard "Yes, I am here." To her surprise, though, this was the voice of a male. "Sir, what's going on there? What can I do to help you?"

At this point, without hanging up, the man put the telephone down and began to wrestle with the girlfriend. The 911 dispatcher could hear exactly what was going on in the house through the telephone. She radioed in and the service people hurried to the scene in their numbers.

While the camera kept rolling, I sank into my sofa and began to wonder and ask myself what may have caused this young man to snap at this early hour of the day. As my mind began to race, seeking answers, my whole being was overcome by a repressive blanket of hopelessness and paranoia. A countless number of reasons flooded my mind as I tried to create understanding, meaning, and answers, I began to reason to myself:

"May be these two had had children and they were having problems in their marriage. May be she has threatened to leave him and he freaking out, decided to annihilate the whole family. May be he was either on drugs or alcohol of both. May be things were not going well at work. In frustration, he decided to vent his anger and disappointment on his girlfriend and children."

Alternatively, I surmised to myself: "It might have been the case that their children were not doing well at school and he was disappointed with the school system. And since he didn't know exactly what the reasons were he blamed the girlfriend for the failure of the children at school and proceeded to hurt her. Or may be since he did not think that the teachers and school authorities could help, he thought it fitting to harass his girlfriend taking the matter into his own hands."

"Yet, I wasn't sure about the validity of any of these concocted reasons. But my mind continued to race, seeking further answers. And the next time I took a look at the television screen this man was coming out of the building with his hands held up. To my relief and happiness, I heard him say repeatedly as he walked toward the police: "I did no harm to her. She is fine. Please don't shoot me. I just don't know what came over me. I..."

At this point, the police hurriedly and roughly handcuffed and thrust him into the back seat of one of the police cruisers. As they read him his rights, he continued to mumble more words to the police regarding the current recession and how he had lost his job. He mentioned that his feelings of emptiness, uselessness, and hopelessness brought him to this point. He was, therefore really mad at everybody. He noted that he could not understand why no social institutions seem to work as efficiently as we desire (Table 1.1). By this point, he was wailing and shedding tears like a little baby whose mom had just left him momentary and he so dearly wanted her attention and affection back. He mumbled about how the failure of government, family, marriage, education, the law, and religion have all failed and creating more problems than they are expected to solve.

Table 1.1: Basic Social Institutions and a Selection of Some of Their Secondary Agencies

Six Basic Social Institutions	Secondary Agencies
1. Politics and Government Operations 2. Family: Marriage, Divorce, and Child Raising 3. Education: Its Direction, Quality, and Reform 4. In the Design and Enforcement of the Law 5. Religion: Spiritual Life and Clergy Performance 6. Economics and Business: Directions and Operations	1. Hospitals 2. Technological Companies 3. Theaters 4. Day Cares for Children 5. Hospices for Adults 6. Communications Tools 7. Entertainments Outlets 8. Immigration and Customs 9. Recovery Facilities (e.g., Alcoholism and drug addiction) 10. Civil Society Organizations 11. Government Organizations Non-Governmental Organizations

When a reporter came closer to the police and asked about what the man said to them, they noted that he was confused and distraught about the various problems that have descended on our society today. He talked about how schools are failing, the corruption in business, government, and even professional organizations. He complained about the financial scandals that make Chief Executive Officers (CEOs) and Chief Financial Officers (CFOs) rich at the expense of everybody else. He complained bitterly about how these people's habitual acts of fraudulence undermine the hardworking employees and jeopardize the little savings they had accumulated toward their retirement years and nobody was doing anything about their situation. Understandably, he was recently out of employment because his company went bankrupt as a result of financial scandals. He complained about the escalation of marital infidelity and wanted to know why nothing was being done to deal with it. He was tired of shooting in schools, restaurants, homes, and workplaces.

According to the police report, one of his greatest frustrations is about how leaders and other elected public officials make great promises and never keep them. They surround themselves with people who possess great academic knowledge and yet are lousy consultants. They offer recommendations for public as well as business policies and plans that usually never work in the long-term. One consultant after another, they all come in and leave, with little impact on company productivity, profitability, and longevity.

To him, we seem to know much and yet gain little from the knowledge we have. Sadly too, without pausing to reflect on why everything we try fails most of the time, we are contented with the usual agenda of gaining more knowledge we neither understand nor are able to use. We create new educational programs at all levels of schooling. We thrust our children into these programs momentarily only to realize that they do not work. The problems these programs were designed and implemented to solve remain and re-emerge in various other ways with cruel and unforgiving vengeance. The social institutions are hurting badly and failing in droves. Where will all this end? Will we lose everything we have worked for throughout our whole lives?

We make new laws and increase the operational budget to enforce them. We are convinced that the new laws will save us. We create tall rules regarding the number of times a criminal has to commit heinous crimes before being put away for good. When any new crimes are committed we run around like chicken without a head, trying to close any legal loopholes. For us it is a race against time. For the most recent victim and family, it is a lost cause. May be, we think to ourselves, the new legal manoeuvres will work. It does not take too long for our jaws to drop in disbelief; another criminal has done it again, even beaten the system, got away scotch free, and proven to us that we are helplessly ignorant about what it takes to lead without failing. In other cases, it is either a CEO or CFO who had either embezzled or misapplied a tremendous amount of money and by so doing jeopardized the retirement funds of the subordinates.

He is taken into an incarceration facility where he lives happily ever after! Or maybe the culprit is a government official who illegally took funds from businesses with the purpose of either selling information to them about intended government plans and policies or to influence the outcome of an upcoming election. In other cases, it is either a revered religious leader who has fallen into the pit of moral doldrums or a law enforcement agent who has be found guilty of several acts of sexual harassment. Worst of all, it is not uncommon to hear of cases regarding spousal/child abuse cases that are heart-stopping. Spousal cheating and deception is common all around us.

What else must we talk about except that the social institutions have all failed and have little to offer? Where must we go from here? Is there any bright light at the end of this dark tunnel of the perennial failure of the social institutions we create to assist us to be on top of the challenges we face daily? Though I do not have any exciting answers to any of these questions, I am keenly aware that we have become experts in a legal solution that does not work as well as he expects. Yet, soon after a new bill has been signed into law, we learn and perceive rather quickly that we must make more stringent laws to either prop up or strengthen the existing ones. We live in a jungle of laws covering almost every sphere of our lives. Yet we are continually failing to make an effective headway in dealing with the prevailing social, economic, political, educational, family, and religious challenges we face.

Worst of all though our star of technological brilliance shines in infinite directions, its fruits are not as satiating as we anticipate. We create technology to help up to transcend our problems. Sooner or later, it becomes a heavy yoke chained around our writs, ankles, necks, and waists. We continue to have a bitter-sweet relationship with our technological innovations and gadgets. Immediately a new technological innovation appears, most of us embrace it with glee and excitement. We give it excellent and raving reviews. Sooner or later, we become aware and familiar with it downside and how its innovators use it to milk us of our hard earned financial resources. Wow, are we stuck or not? Where do all these lead us? Is there a way out?

Our technological and scientific brilliance is yet to enhance our effectiveness in dealing with health challenges that dog us today. We seek challenges to these through our unshakable faith in science and technology. We have become convinced that most of health problems are genetic and can only be dealt with through technological inventions and/or innovations. The air of excellence we exude does not seem to yield the expected fruits. The academic brilliance we have attained does not seem to show the way either. Or should I say that even when we discover new knowledge and do not know exactly how to make the best use of it, we abandon it and continue on to channel tremendous amounts of our scarce financial, effort, energy, and time (FEET) resources into other new research opportunities. These practices bring to mind a nagging question: What do we actually want?

Though mediocrity is the order of the day, we claim to be doing our best under the circumstances. Like distraught ostriches, we stop running midway and burry our heads in the sand, and thinking that our problems have disappeared since we no longer see them. Worst of all, we do not lack professional managerial and leadership consultants. This genre of people is over-supplied. They give excellent seminars and conferences during which they thrill us as their audiences to heightened emotional feelings and great expectations. They are vibrant and inspirational. When we listen to them we become convinced that we too can successfully turn around the negative tides that engulf our own organizations, lives, expectations, and avoid any more potential hardships.

And yet when we return from these seminars to our organizations/places of work and try any of these new knowledge, techniques, and how-to-do-it-yourself ideas only those among us who are fortunate make only temporal progress. But this gain wilts quickly, leaving them confused as to why the ideas learned from the great leaders and managers of our basic social institutions don't work. The buckets of knowledge and recommendations that ooze out of the lips of our highly reverenced sages placed in charge of leading, managing, and running our social institutions are impotent. Though we willingly accept and freely consume this new pool of information drawn from these people, we are again back to square one. As a result, we have to go out again and again to contract with a brand new group of management gurus that has recently come into town.

The reality of continuing failures brings pertinent questions that demand attention and answers: Why is our continuing exposure to new information and knowledge not leading us to deal effectively with the problems and challenges that confront us in our social institutions? What are we either missing or doing wrong? What must we do to succeed? Until we find workable answers to each of these questions and others like them we will flounder and fail on the shores of illusion. Our social institutions will always remain in their ineffectiveness and waddle in their perennial failures. Should this become our plight, we truly are in a serious predicament as we travel individually and as group through life.

The Human Predicament

As we reflect more deeply on these observations and the associated questions posed, it dawns on us that the human predicament is vividly captured in a reflection note that arrived in my e-mailbox from a colleague on Friday, July 2, 1999 at 15: 29:51 hours. I am not sure of its precise origin and author. Its title is: *The Truth of the Matter.* Without mincing any words, the author observes:

The paradox of our time in history is that we have taller buildings, but shorter tempers; wider freeways, but narrower viewpoints. We spend more, but have less; we buy more, but enjoy it less. We have bigger houses and smaller families; more conveniences, but less time; we have more degrees, but less sense; more knowledge, but less judgment; more experts, but more problems; more medicine, but less wellness. We drink too much, smoke too much, spend too recklessly, laugh too little, drive too fast, get too angry too quickly, stay up too late, get up too tired, read too seldom, watch TV too much, and pray too seldom. We have multiplied our possessions, but reduced our values.

We talk too much, love too seldom, and hate too often. We've learned how to make a living, but not a life; we've added years to life, not life to years. We've been all the way to the moon and back, but have trouble crossing the street to meet the new neighbour. We've conquered outer space, but not inner space. We've done larger things, but not better things. We've cleaned up the air, but polluted the soul. We've split the atom, but not our prejudice. We write more, but learn less. We plan more, but accomplish less. We've learned to rush, but not to wait. We build more computers to hold more information to produce more copies than ever, but have less communication. These are the times of fast foods and slow digestion; tall men, and short character; steep profits, and shallow relationships.

These are the times of world peace, but domestic warfare; more leisure, but less fun; more kinds of food, but less nutrition. These are days of two incomes, but more divorce; of fancier houses, but broken homes. These are days of quick trips, disposable diapers, throw-away morality, one-night stands, overweight bodies, and pills that do everything from cheer to quiet, to kill. It is a time when there is much in the show window and nothing in the stockroom; a time when technology can bring this letter to you, and a time when you can choose either to share this insight, or to just hit delete.

Well, as a result of the recommendation to either choose to hit the delete button or share this insight with orders, I receive the unrestricted permission to share this great freely message by bringing it to the attention of my readers in this book.

Humanity is at the verge of collapse because we continue to elect the path of that produces quick and unsustainable results. We are running on a full tank of gas and at our fastest speed ever only to realize that we are spinning the wheels of our vehicle of life on a stationary treadmill. Though the horse that powers and pulls our vehicle of life shows signs of death, instead of dismounting, a wise thing to do, we contract with management consultants and immerse ourselves in a leadership style that recommends to us to continue on with the ride and blocking out of our minds that the horse has actually died!

We will return to this practice and discuss it in Chapter 6. Conferences, conferences, conferences! We call for more seminars and round table discussion sessions. We create new committees to research and bring recommendations to us. We sit around tiny tables in coffee shops all around us and engage in serious brainstorming sessions as to what our next action regarding how to increase the bottom line must be. We sign up for new training sessions regarding how to discover our strengths and by so doing part ourselves in the back by not worrying about our weaknesses. Yet, when the rubber meets the road the play out of these weaknesses trumps the power of our strengths. For while our strengths are organized around our knowledge, skills, and abilities, our weaknesses are founded in and informed by the universal spiritual and moral principles we most frequently either ignore or reject without impunity.

Undeniably, our spiritual and moral weaknesses *ALWAYS* trump the intellectual strengths we possess in every regard. We are at the top of the knowledge hill. Yet we suffer acutely from the *syndrome of analysis of paralysis*. These realities about our living and plight bring another relevant question: Why is the quest for more knowledge not redeeming us?

Though working diligently with great conviction, we cover no additional distance. At best, we get more and more tired; obnoxiously agitated; helplessly furious; and hopelessly worn out. We do everything to the best of our abilities with the hope of achieving and sustaining happiness. Yet, happiness seems to be too slippery an animal to pin down. It eludes us every moment we think to ourselves we have nailed it down. We often feel we are just about to catch it; only to perceive that by the time we get back into the comfort of our own houses, it has already slipped away. The gifts we give and receive in return make us dissatisfied, angrier, joyless, and sadder than ever. We sign up for more academic degree programs and other forms of amusement, trusting that they will make us feel better and more successful.

We create many more civil society groups, non-profit organizations, governmental organizations, and non-governmental organizations. We set up new and specialized clinics, half-way-houses, hospices, hospitals, research institutes, professional associations, multicultural rendezvous to comfort ourselves, community discussion groups/sessions, and others like these. We engage in new educational and training programs to enhance our knowledge base, sharpen our skills, and hone our strengths.

Yet, right on graduation day, when the excitement of having completed another academic degree program has already got worn off, our realities unquestionably dampen the spirit and the anxiety we feel blankets us. These phenomena steal the desired happiness away from us and ruin the victory dance we had planned for. We become acutely depressed and few people know why. We turn to artificial stimulants such as drugs, alcohol, food, entertainment, and other forms of vulgar practices. The emptiness and the nagging feelings of failure and sadness we experience reside within us. And when we gather with experts who claim to know the answers they only make our situation worse. The counsel we receive from them is most frequently empty and depressing; exacerbating our feelings of failure, helplessness, and hopelessness. We expectantly await this counsel and its diagnoses of the situation so we can bring order into the crisis and chaos around us. The prescription is to numb the pain and advocate solutions that lead to the self-realization that one must just accept what life has dealt them. So we hit the road and play the harlot with drugs, alcohol, and any form of entertainment we can possibly drum up. We only do any of these when it makes us feel good momentarily.

The Way Forward

It is undeniably true that through a thorough reflection on the realities presented in the forgoing paragraphs we have gained a better understanding of our predicaments. What we must now do is to become committed to digging deeper to decipher the knowledge chest we already possess on a daily basis. Working diligently together, we can craft precisely new and better solutions we require to break the backbone of our perennial problems of lack of understanding, ignorance, and ability to apply the knowledge learned toward the effectiveness of our social institutions (Table 1.1).

But to accomplish this task successfully, we must commit to work diligently to transition from the initial stage of knowledge (information) acquisition to wisdom through understanding. Without being successful at this virtuously progressive process, we will remain forever stuck in the vicious cycle of leadership/managerial failures and declining quality of life.

It is my desire to point and guide us to the starting point where we can regroup and then begin to act with the purpose of transcending the vicious cycle of leadership failures that have pushed us into making bad decisions in the past. The primary objective of this book is not to explain the significance of the quality of the human factor to the inefficiencies we experience in the operations of the social institutions. To understand this, we will highlight its role in corporate corruption and its implications for the future contributions of our social institutions. The human factor refers to:

The spectrum of personality characteristics and other dimensions of human performance that enable social, economic, and political institutions to function, and remain functional, over time. Such dimensions sustain the workings and application of the rule of law, political harmony, disciplined labour force, just legal systems, respect for human dignity and the sanctity of life, social welfare, and so on. As is often the case, no social, economic, or political institutions can function effectively without being upheld by a network of committed persons who stand firmly by them. Such persons must strongly believe in, and continually affirm, ideals of society (Adjibolosoo, 1995, p. 83).

.With this definition for the human factor in mind, the main argument in this book is that no nation can make its economy work efficiently for long without having honed the positive qualities of the human factor.

The book is not about the basic everyday reasons why people fail in personal relationships, business ventures, economic activities, or community assignments. Above all, I am not proposing which leadership theories and models make more sense than others. Neither is this book written to confirm or validate the views of certain scholars of leadership theory and disapprove the ideas of others. The contents of this book are not about the *how-tos* of leadership effectiveness in the social institutions through the *dos* and *don'ts* of problem-solving techniques.

Instead, in light of the observations present in this chapter, it is argued in the remainder of this book that leadership development with the social institutions in mind *must transcend mere knowledge and skill acquisition and concentrate primarily on the development of the positive qualities of the human factor*. The recognition that the quality of the human factor is the key pillar of leadership effectiveness will move individuals beyond what they dreamed possible.

Leadership success or failure in any social institution is affected by *the real self*, who the leader is as a person, and those he or she works with. The qualities of a leader's human factor as well as those of the subordinates bring tremendous impact to bear on the attitudes, actions, and effectiveness of the individuals within the social institutions. Specifically, the contents of this book provide a new dimension to the existing recommended solutions to leadership and managerial failures prevalent in the social institutions. The application of the knowledge and insight presented in this book will strengthen our combined resolve and abilities to discover new and better ways to enhance our own personal leadership development program and effectiveness in the social institutions. By so doing, every one of us will begin to work diligently toward a total transformation that will catapult us into becoming the kind of leader and/or manager he have always dreamed of becoming. As Albert Einstein states it, "Try not to become a man of success but rather to become a man of value."

The contents of this book are aimed at guiding every one of us to learn, know, and apply the knowledge and recommendations toward the individual as well as the corporate minimization of the intensity of leadership and managerial failures and continual problems in the social institutions. By so doing, we will improve the quality of life for ourselves and all others who too are bold enough to follow in our footsteps.

I must add, though, that since the human factor-based solution is identical to the efficiency of every one of the social institution, my election is to concentrate essentially on only one of the basic social institutions whose activities lead to the financial refuelling of all the others and their subsidiaries. The decision to use the economy as a very vital institution is based on the fact that our activities in it provide us with the financial as well as all the other factors of production we require to succeed. Your understanding of the presentations, using the economy as a powerful example, will guide you to understand better why all the other social institutions do not do well when the economy is in a recession/depression. Every time you read the title of this book, *The Human Factor Foundation of Free Market Efficiency*, you can easily change it to reflect the social institution in which you work. For example, if you work for the government, your book's title is: *The Human Factor Foundation of Government Efficiency*. Every other person who works for any other social institution can create their own title accordingly.

Primary Objective of this Book

In light of the foregoing presentations, this book outlines the theory and empirical evidence about *the human factor foundation of free market efficiency*. The contents of this book primarily show that the sole variable that underscores the degree of efficiency the *laissez-faire* economic system experiences is determined by the quality of the human factor of those who engage in business practices and income generating economic activities. Throughout the centuries the critical knowledge about that which makes the free market economic system function efficiently has been a mystery. Few economists, business owners, managers, and political leaders are aware of what makes the free market economic system function effectively and remain functional over time.

The primary thrust of this book is three-fold. *First*, it is argued that few scholars or ordinary citizens understand the real factor that causes and ameliorates economic downturns. *Secondly*, it is argued that until we know and understand the actual source of any economic recessions and depressions, we cannot deal with them effectively. *Thirdly*, it is concluded that the true foundation of an efficiently functioning free market economic system is a virtuous blend of the positive as well as the negative qualities of the human factor.

Organization of the Book

The remainder of the book is organized in the following manner. The discussions presented in Chapter 2 highlight the significance of economics to dealing with the economizing problem in society. Chapter 3 focuses on unhindered pursuits of self-interests and the wealth creation process. Chapter 4 discusses some of the key assumptions of orthodox economic theorizing. Chapter 5 focuses on the genesis of the unfolding of our economic problems and the new challenges they breed. Chapter 6 concentrates on the sources of our inaction in dealing effectively with the economic problems that face us and the resulting failure. Chapter 7 presents observations made from the critical issues presented and discussed in Chapters 2 through 5. Chapter 8 focuses on the definition of the human factor and its relevance to human action in every sphere of life. Chapter 9 concentrates on a presentation that deals with today's economic challenges: the ebb and flow of economic activities in the free market system. In Chapter 10 is the presentation and analyses of the foundation of free market efficiency. In this Chapter arguments are made regarding the importance of the quality of the human factor to the economic challenges we face today. In Chapter 11 are concepts and ideas put forward toward the development of the positive qualities of the human factor. In Chapter 12 are the conclusions and recommendations for public policy.

It is my hope that the applications you make of the knowledge you gain through your reading of this book will lead you to improve the quality of your own life and those of others who interact and work with you. You will place yourself in a vantage position from which you will leading and/or manage others to succeed in the social institution within which you work. Your own successes will also make it possible for your subordinates to optimize their own effectiveness in the various positions they find themselves in their own organizations.

And when this is our combine reality, we will succeed in enhancing our own individual quality of life and those of others who too depend on us. Sooner or later, this world will become a better place for every human being. We will then leave a worthwhile legacy for our children and their children's children, eternally. What an excellent vision to have and live for!

2

Significance of Economics for Economizing Problem

Let us begin with a basic understanding of what led to the evolution of economic systems and their significance to economic theorizing. This knowledge will guide us in the rest of the book as we take up the challenge of gaining a deeper understanding of the economic challenges we have faced. By mastering this knowledge, we will understand how our perennial failures have denied us the opportunity and ability to deal with the primary source of the economic problems of the past and those that continue to plague us today.

In this chapter the reader will become more familiar with what economics is, its reason for being an academic discipline, and the purposes for which it was fashioned. Our deeper understanding of the primary thrust of economics as an academic discipline will enhance our appreciation for its existence. It will also guide us to know well why it is an imperative for trained economists, business people, government administrators, members of civil society groups, leaders, managers of organizations, and any other citizens to become familiar with the relevance of the quality of the human factor to the efficiency of the free market economy. As we embark upon our discussions and analyses in this book, it is imperative that we have an excellent understanding of what the word *market*, means in economics.

In economics, a market is any arrangement people make for trading with one another. Viewed in this light, a market is not necessarily a particular physical location one must always go to purchase goods and services. A *market structure* refers to the conditions or characteristics that define the environment within which firms operate. Such structures impact the production and pricing decisions of companies that operating in the market structure. In traditional economic analysis, there are four main market structures. These include *perfect competition* (made up of many small-sized producers or firms), *monopoly* (constituted of one firm only), *monopolistic competition* (has mostly many firms most of which a small in size), and *oligopoly* (this is made up of a combination of few large firms and probably a large number of relatively smaller firms that serve the market on its fringes). Our discussions in this book concentrate on competitive markets in the *laissez-faire* economic system.

Abraham Maslow's Hierarchy of Needs

The decision to engage in the study of any academic discipline requires that one focus on its core knowledge, become familiar with its language, acquire the skills and abilities required to use this language, understand the importance of the discipline to humanity, and be able to apply every one of these to problem solving.

The one critical question everyone interested in the discipline of economics must seek meaningful answers to is: "Why do human beings engage in economic activities?" To ascertain answers to this question, we must recall Abraham Maslow's (1943 and 1954) view regarding the kinds of needs humans have and how they go about satisfying them. According to Maslow, human needs can be classified as biological and physiological, safety, belongingness, esteem, self-actualized, and higher level longings such as spiritual and moral fulfilment. Let us proceed to provide brief descriptions for each of these needs.

1. **Biological and Physiological Needs:** These needs relate to the acquisition and enjoyment of the basic necessities of life such as food, clothing, and shelter. Others include the satisfaction of personal emotional feelings, having good sleep, warmth, emotional cravings, and other kinds of sensual needs and desires.

2. **Safety Needs:** Enjoying security, protection, order, and stability. Protection from and through the law is expected in addition to these.

3. **Belongingness Needs:** Feeling and experiencing the love and affection of family members and friends. Having and enjoying excellent relationships in one's circle of friends and influence. It also includes the personal experiences of caring, nurturing, and growth.

4. **Esteem Needs:** This need relates to personal achievements, attained status in life, earned responsibilities, accountabilities, and reputations.

5. **Self-Actualization Needs:** This need speaks to the personal achievement of growth and fulfilment in diverse spheres of personal life.

6. **Higher Level Longings such as Spiritual and Moral Fulfilment Needs:** This need is about satisfying the feelings of personal transcendence. It is about rising higher and above the personal desire for and commitment to the satisfaction of the basic necessities of life. It is being able to enjoy lifestyle choices propelled by the personal desire to live according to the universal spiritual and moral principles of life.

Arguably, the desire to satisfy these needs provides the motivation to engage in income generating activities. We create businesses to generate income. We use these acquired financial resources and other forms of wealth to meet the array of needs we have.

Regardless of the degree to which any of these needs is satisfied, the current level of satisfaction never carries over to the next moment. That is, few biological and physiological needs can be satisfied once for one's entire lifespan. We have to continually satisfy each of these desires throughout our whole lifespan. Any desire which has just been satisfied is only for the moment. Sooner or later, this desire returns and views for immediate attention and satisfaction again and again and...For example, we are only able to temporarily satisfy our feelings of hunger and other sensual desires. That is, a few hours later, after a certain desire has been already satisfied in the moment, it shows up again and again and again...demanding that it be satisfied. As a result, we neither can ignore the calls of hunger nor cease from engaging in economic activities for as long as we are alive. When we become incapacitated in any form, we need others to generate sufficient income so they can take adequate care of us. Undeniably, therefore, we are perennially needy in diverse ways!

Growing from infants into childhood we have parents, loved ones, and friends who take care of most of our basic needs of food, clothing, and shelter. But as we grow older and engage in social, economic, educational, political, and technological endeavours, we realize that we must be involved in certain income-generating activities to satisfy the needs we have. Though we can temporarily control and even possibly delay the satisfaction of some of our biological needs, we cannot totally ignore them forever. As we mature into adulthood we pursue economic and business activities to generate more income required to pay for the goods and services we must have to satisfy all our desires. Much of what we do is driven by individual desires and self-interests. We become excited about the self-interests we have. We also possess strong desires and commitment to pursue income generating activities to fulfil our basic as well as the higher level spiritual and moral needs.

Beyond these needs, whether or not we are aware of it, we also crave the satisfaction of our higher spiritual and moral fulfilment. These feelings are deeply rooted in our core of inner being. When they are left unfulfilled, even the affluence we have acquired is unable to bring us the happiness, joy, peace, and harmony we so desperately want. The lack of satisfaction of these higher level needs forces some individuals to go on a lifetime quest to discover that which can give them personal satisfaction. Biographies of people as well as other kinds of empirical evidence have revealed that the quest for personal happiness leads some individuals to the path of entertainment in diverse spheres of life. Some examples of practices aimed at personal satisfaction include sports, movies, comedies, singing, and dancing. To these activities, some people on this quest engage in diverse sexual practices and/or orientations. Others sell their feelings and desires to alcohol and drugs. Those who can afford it chase after and engage in expensive hobbies, compulsive eating, dieting practices, exercising, and travel.

Importance of the Study of Economics

Every person has personal reasons for participating in income generating activities and the many ways the financial resources are used. We seek financial stability through business and other economic activities. Yet regardless of how we view our attitudes and actions, there are two distinct but unspoken objectives for pursuing these economic activities. First, for some people the primary motives are clearly in pursuit of their *self-interests* to gain personal respect, fame, and self-gratification. The actions of these people at the marketplace are aimed at solely maximizing their financial resources to attain the highest possible satisfaction (i.e., *utility*) level. For this group of people, their participation in economic and business activities is an end in itself. These people view the pursuit of self-interests as the only real objective for their exertion in the free market economy.

Second, others pursue self-interests to jointly fulfil both the lower and the higher level needs. They are guided by the universal spiritual and moral principles toward the pursuit of their self-interests. For these people sound ethical decision-making and uncompromised moral behaviours and actions in the marketplace are paramount. They see themselves as stewards of the resources they acquire in the marketplace. Members of this group perceive their pursuit of self-interests as a means to an end. But the participation in income generating activities at the marketplace is an act aimed at the maximization of their incomes and how to use it to fulfil their spiritual, moral, social, physiological, educational, psychological, and technological needs.

Two Possible Outcomes of the Drama of Human Life

There are two possible outcomes of these diverse human experiences in terms of the pursuit of self-interests. For most people, the array of human experiences is defined on a linear scale. This scale ranges from the experiences of the *good life* at one end of the spectrum and those of the *bad life* at the other end. Between these two extremes is a diversity of lifetime experiences that are mixtures of both. Some are closer to the good life than to the bad life. Of course, we must keep in mind that even that which constitutes the good or bad life is not easily defined! The variety of human experiences is infinite. Regardless of the kind and quality of life we live, everyone ultimately experiences physical death. Although no one knows exactly what happens to us after death, there are debates regarding whether there exists any other forms of life hereafter.

For example, some people are convinced that physical death results in the loss of all memory of living. When we die, everything about us ceases to be and there is nothing hereafter. Everything about us is erased from the memories of those who knew us. Others believe that after death, the spirit and soul live on forever. In this case those people who believe in the existence of God or a higher power maintain that a final day of judgment will ensue at some point in time. They argue that after death the human spirit and/or soul experience(s) eternal glory or damnation depending upon how our spirits and souls fare during the final judgment.

Our beliefs regarding that which happens after death require of us to pursue our self-interests in manners congruent with our views of eternity. During our earthly life we go about engaging in many different kinds of activities. We act in our best self-interests on the universal stage of the cosmos. Such personal acts and performances aimed at the satisfaction of our daily needs define the nature and quality of our social, economic, political, educational, and technological lives.

What then is Economics?

Viewed from a principle-cantered perspective, it is arguable that in the drama of economic and business life, each individual serves other humans as a responsible person in order to earn some income with which to care for himself or herself and other dependants, if there are any. This reality or practice brings to mind the question: "What then is economics?

Succinctly stated, *economics is the social science which focuses on the study of people's behaviours and actions in regard to the acquisition, distribution, and use of their available scarce financial, effort, energy, and time (FEET) resources with the sole purpose of attaining and sustaining the maximum level of satisfaction.* Traditionally the main economic resources that are channelled into the production process are referred to as the factors of production. These factors of production include land, labour, capital, and the entrepreneur. While the returns to land are referred to as rent, that to labour is wage or salary. The return to capital is called interest. The entrepreneur receives the residual or profits. This is why we usually refer to the entrepreneur as the residual claimant.

It is the limited nature of the factors of production leads to the creation of what economists refer to as the economizing problem. This problem is indicative of how our needs exceed the means with which we can satisfy and also sustain them on a daily basis. Almost all of our needs, as noted earlier, are recurrent throughout our individual lifespan.

Economizing Problem and Economic Systems

One of the greatest challenges we face is the fact that

while our needs are unlimited, the FEET resources with which to satisfy each need are limited. The variance between our needs and the ability to satisfy each one of them forms the basis of what economists refer to as *the economizing problem*. The economizing problem is also referred to as *scarcity, the limited nature of our productive FEET resources*. The painful reality of scarcity requires that we make *wise choices* regarding how we elect to employ our limited FEET resources to satisfy pressing needs. *Choice* is about having to select because the number of wants we have and desire to satisfy far exceeds the available FEET resources with which to acquire them all.

However, once we make any particular choice, we incur *an opportunity cost*. Opportunity cost is defined as the forgone alternative(s) of the choices we make in real rather than monetary terms. Undeniably, choices have costs. These costs relate to what is sacrificed once a choice is made. That is, the foregone alternative is the actual physical item foregone rather than its true monetary value.

Suppose, for example, that Abla, a girl, is at the moment dating four boys whose names are Senyo, Sena, Setor, and Seli. When Abla decides finally to accept Senyo's proposal for marriage, she cannot accept and marry Sena or Setor or Seli at the same time—except she lives in a polyandrous society! Abla forgoes these other three men to marry Senyo. The real costs to Abla for choosing Senyo as her prospective husband are the other three guys whose proposals she had previously rejected. It is important to know that when the magnitude of the true opportunity cost changes, our attitudes, behaviours, and actions change accordingly, The lower the opportunity costs, the larger the probability that we will make the decision to engage in a particular attitude, behaviour, and action. Alternatively, when the perceived opportunity cost is huge, there is a less desire to pursue any of the contemplated attitudes, behaviours, and actions.

Critical Fundamental Economic Questions

The presence of the reality of scarcity, choice, opportunity cost, and unintended consequences of the choices we make brings to light a set of foundational questions in economics. Among these queries are (1) What is to be produced? (2) How is it to be produced? (3) When will it be produced? (4) For whom is it produced? (5) How will it be produced? Each of these queries is explained briefly below:

1. **What is to be produced?** This question relates to the allocation of the available scarce FEET resources to be channelled into the production of each commodity.

2. **How is it to be produced?** This query speaks to the kinds of technology to be employed in the production process.

3. **When will it be produced?** This question highlights the significance of the time horizon within which the commodity is to be produced. In economics there are three kinds of time horizons related to the production process. The first one is referred to as the short-run. This time horizon is solely a representation of the producer's ability to change some inputs (i.e., the variable inputs) and the inability to do so for others (i.e., fixed inputs). The second one is referred to as the long-run. In the long-run, the producer has the capability to alter every possible input used in the production process. However, the producer is unable to alter the technology in current use. The third time horizon is referred to as the very long-run. In the very long run, the producer is able to vary every input, including technology too. The caveat, though, is that in the very long-run, we may all be dead! This is because those who initiate any innovative/inventive ideas do not necessarily carry it to its ultimate fruition within their full lifespan. This is left to members of future generations to do.

4. **For whom is it produced?** The answer to this question is related to the people for whom the commodity has been produced. That is, this question is about having knowledge

of the people who will patronize and consume the commodity. Since there are scarce economic resources, the producer is interested in knowing whether to channel these FEET resources into the production of goods and services for infants, children, adolescents, adults, or senior citizens. Other considerations include gender, race, students, and any other distinguishing features. Producers are not interested in creating items where there is no market for them!

5. **How will it be distributed?** This final query concentrates on the identification of the methods or procedures the commodity will be allotted to or acquired by the citizens. It speaks about who the end users are. This question is also about ownership and how each individual acquires the commodity in question. For example, will the commodity in question be given to people as a free gift? Or will people pay money to acquire it? Will it be distributed freely on the basis of first come, first served; or do people have to engage in wrestling or boxing matches with the winners earning the right to receive and consume the commodity? This is a very important question for the production process as far as the use of scarce FEET resources is concerned.

Economic Systems

As we participate in the drama of life in the theatre of the cosmos, our desire is to minimize the economizing problem. We realize this is what led our forefathers to devise methodologies aimed at guiding them, us, and our offspring to make the most efficient and prudent use of the available scarce FEET resources. In economic theory these techniques which have been fashioned throughout the centuries to minimize the impact of the scarcity problem are what we refer to today as *Economic Systems*. It is the human search for answers to each of these important questions that led to the design and operation of the various economic systems.

In our study of economics we must be aware that the reality of the economizing problem leads us to design a diversity of *rationing devices* to assist us in the day-to-day pursuits of our self-interests. A rationing device is an allocation technique. It helps us to determine how to distribute the goods and services we produce. Scarcity induces competition. It is the primary purpose why we compete for the kinds of rationing devices we use in our economy. Regardless of whether we know it or not, every one attempts to make decisions at the margin. To make a decision at the margin is to think in terms of additional or marginal benefits and costs that emerge as we contemplate taking a particular action.

For example, suppose there are three different routes A, B, and C to travel from Akatsi to Accra, the capital city of Ghana. Suppose further that while route A has constant police presence, route B has frequent delays due to road construction and maintenance work. Route C has cattle, goats, sheep, and fowls crossing at various locations at intervals. If you had to select any one of these routes to travel from Akatsi to Accra, which one of these routes would you choose? Simply stated, your decision will be affected by your expected net marginal benefits. That is, you will choose the route that promises the highest net gain to you. This represents the route that gives you the greatest benefit at the most minimal cost! Factors that may feature prominently in your decision making process include miles per gallon, number of stops, the average speed of travel time per hour, and personal comfort. Your choice of route is finally based on your expected net marginal gain! In addition to these there exists the reality of unintended effects or consequences of decisions made.

Types of Economic Systems

There are two major modern economic systems. These are *Capitalism* and *Socialism*. The capitalist economic system is frequently referred to as *the free enterprise system, the laissez faire economic system,* or *the free market economic system.*

The socialistic economic system is labelled in various ways as *command economic system, a hierarchical economic system,* or *government regulated economic system.* Since there is actually no nation that is strictly capitalistic or socialistic, we talk about a third economic system. It is referred to as the Mixed Economic System. This third economic system is a hybrid of capitalism and socialism. It assumes certain characteristics of both capitalism and socialism.

Contrary to popularly help opinion among trained economists as well as non-trained economists, the foundation of any economic system is the quality of the people's human factor. To understand the effectiveness of any economic system, one must understand the role the quality of people's human factor quality plays in their pursuits of self-interests. We will present and discuss these issues in later chapters.

3

Pursuits of Self-Interest and the Wealth Creation Process

Having dwelt on Planet Earth for centuries and transitioned through countless generations, few people have known and understood the critical factor that provides for an unshakable foundation and performance of the free market economic system. Though most classical or neoclassical economists argue that the *laissez-faire* economic system is superior to all others, especially the socialist economic system and the communism it engenders, few of these scholars possess the understanding of how the free market economic system works.

This lack of knowledge makes it impossible for anyone to understand the primary source of and also deal effectively with recessions or depressions when they happen. Attempts to mitigate the severe impact of such economic downturns are based on ignorance, fear of loss of personal wealth, and panic attacks that emerge from confusion. Together these realities trigger an avalanche of avid commitment to the pursuit of trial-and-error methods rather than mounting a diligent and an aggressive search for and the discovery of applications drawn from the possession of relevant knowledge and understanding. Throughout the centuries, humans have experienced diverse forms and different levels of severity of economic recessions and depressions. There was a devastatingly traumatic recession in the 1930s after the crashing of the stock market in 1929. Thereafter there have been minor forms of recessions over the decades. Worthy of note in our recent economic history were those recessions that occurred in 1973, 1983, 1990, and 2001.

When the global economy began to slip into a serious recessionary tailspin in 2007 and finally climaxed into a full-blown economic devastation in 2008, government leaders from all over the world responded with diverse economic recovery and bailout packages. This kind of move was carried out swiftly and it quickly became pervasive elsewhere in the Global Village. No time was wasted by political leaders and social activists regarding the design and implementation of economic recovery programs in the developed countries.

Unfortunately every one of these mitigating programs was nothing more than short-term quick-fixes and problem-accommodating gestures based on rugged feelings and trial and error mentality. Given the results to date, these attempts have left most people vulnerable to the existing challenges and their uncertain future. What most economists, business people, organizational leaders, and government administrators fail to understand is the real root cause of economic recessions and/or depressions. If only members of each of these groups will read and understand Adam Smith's perspectives on the *laissez-faire* economic system, they will become better-prepared to deal effectively with recessions and/or depressions; or may be even pre-empt and either stop them far ahead of time or minimize the intensity of their impact.

To proceed further into our discussions and analyses in this book, let us get ourselves acquainted with Adam Smith's perspective on the real source of economic efficiency and weaknesses. In his first book entitled *The Theory of Moral Sentiments (1759)*, Adam Smith, the Father of economics, laid down in no uncertain terms the significance of the moral foundations of the *laissez-faire* economic system. His presentations in the second book, *An Inquiry into the Nature and Causes of the Wealth of Nations (1776)*, built on the contents of the first book.

When taken together, the contents of both books reveal that the *laissez-faire* economic system will never attain its optimal level of efficiency in the absence of the commitment market agents make to pursue and practice higher moral standards in their pursuits of self-interests. According to Adam

Smith the prevalence of and respect for *natural liberty* in any society require a people who are committed to living their lives and participating in free market activities on the basis of strict adherence to moral principles and the standards they mandate. These Smithian perspectives are evident in the pursuit of self-interests within the boundaries of natural liberty.

Unhindered Pursuits of Self-Interests

To understand the Smithian perspective on the pursuit of self-interests which defines the efficiency of the *laissez-faire* economic system as discussed in his second book, *An Inquiry into the Nature and Causes of the Wealth of Nations* (1776), one must be familiar with the contents of his first book, *The Theory of Moral Sentiments* (1759). Those who fail to familiarize themselves with the contents of the *Theory of Moral Sentiments* (1759) are likely to misunderstand Adam Smith's perspective on the significance of self-interest pursuits to free market efficiency.

In the United States and the developed world most academicians and free market agents (i.e., business people) have generally equated the pursuit of self-interests to the pursuance of insatiable selfishness. Yet those who think they do pursue self-interests actually position their attitudes, behaviours, and actions in acts of selfishness instead. This reality only illustrates that these people are unaware of Smith's distinction between the two kinds of self-interests. In the Smithian view the pursuit of self-interests can either be positioned in *principle-centeredness* or *non-principle-centeredness*. The paths of self-interested pursuits that are non-principle-cantered lead to high levels of rapaciousness.

In the long-term these paths of greed promote non-principle-cantered self-interested pursuits that lead to the destruction of the wealth creation process. The reality of this type of self-interests produces continuing decline in business and economic activities within any economic system. It leads to economic stagnation and underdevelopment. This is not the kind of self-interested pursuits Adam Smith lauds.

The type of self-interested pursuits that Adam Smith encourages are those which lead to the expressions of personal attitudes, behaviours, and actions that produce net benefits to the self and to others (Smith, 1759 and 1776). This type of personal pursuits of self-interests is principle-cantered. When carried out in this manner, the pursuits of self-interests bring unintended benefits to other community member too. In the words of Adam Smith (1776),

"It is not from the benevolence of the butcher, the brewer, or the baker that we expect our dinner, but from their regard to their own self-interest. We address ourselves, not to their humanity but to their self-love, and never talk to them of our own necessities but of their advantages...By pursuing his own interest he frequently promotes that of the society more effectually than when he really intends to promote it...How selfish so ever man may be supposed, there are evidently some principles in his nature, which interest him in the fortune of others, and render their happiness necessary to him, though he derives nothing from it, except the pleasure of seeing it."

Adam Smith spells out in no uncertain terms the distinction between principle-cantered and non-principle-cantered self-interests. Yet because most of us are quick to defraud and dispossess others in what we do daily in the various marketplaces, we audaciously equate principle-cantered self-interests to selfishness without giving it any much thought. While locked in this mode, we become convinced that greed is good and therefore practice it in our dealings with others in the free market economic system.

When personal self-interests are pursued in accordance with the desire for making good on principle-cantered lifestyle choices, personal as well as social net gains are achieved and sustained. The expression of honesty produces benefits through self-love and love of neighbour. In the Smithian (1759) perspective, people possess the capacity to love themselves and others equally (see Smith's *The Theory of*

Moral Sentiments, 1759). The expression of these capacities of love in the personal pursuits of self-interests with integrity and respect for other people's rights, self worth, and dignity sustains and enhances the wealth creation process. This practice fosters harmony, tranquillity, and happiness for people. It also magnifies personal achievements in the chosen vocations in the various marketplaces. The economy experiences ongoing virtuous cycles and the whole society benefits.

Thus, as Adam Smith poignantly puts it:

Every individual necessarily labours to render the annual revenue of the society as great as he can. He generally neither intends to promote the public interest, nor knows how much he is promoting it. By preferring the support of domestic industry to that of foreign industry, he intends only his own security; and by directing that industry in such a manner as its produce may be of the greatest value, he intends only his own gain, and he is in this, as many other cases, *led by an invisible hand to promote an end which was no part of his intention*. Nor is it always the worse for the society that it was no part of it...I have never known much good done by those who affected trade for the public good. It is an affectation, indeed, not very common among merchants, and very few words need be employed in dissuading them from it (see Smith, 1776; the emphases are mine).

The pursuits of self-interests are not necessarily required or mandated to be insidiously calculated acts of selfishness intentionally aimed at duping and dispossessing others. If it were so, these selfish intentions will only reflect the ferociously mean and hateful side of our being.

Adam Smith, however, points out that there is that part of our being which is kind, loving, gentle, and honest. The ascendancy of this part of our being is that which promotes and sustains the pursuits of principle-cantered self-interests. While this later kind of self-interested pursuits enhances the wealth of nations, the former diminishes it in the short-run and totally destroys it in the long-run.

Writing his own commentary on the Smithian concept of self-interested pursuits.

The classical economists assumed that self-interested behaviour was basic to human nature. Producers and merchants provided goods and services out of a desire to make profits; workers offered their labour services in order to obtain wages, and consumers purchased products as a way to satisfy their wants...With the important exception of Ricardo, the classicists emphasized the natural harmony of interest in a market economy. By pursuing their own individual interests, people served the best interests of society.

Though Brue's rendition of the concept of self-interests may make a lot of sense to the lay person, it is convoluted. First, Brue fails to tell us about what he considers to be *human nature*; knowing different scholars have different perspectives on this nebulously deceptive concept. Secondly, he is unaware of the Smithian distinction of principle-cantered self-interests and pure selfishness. It is the failure to make this distinction in the *laissez-faire* economic system that misleads market agents to engage in greedy attitudes, behaviours, and actions. And yet they think and believe that they are pursuing their own self-interests. These practices lead the invisible hand astray and subsequently create devastating economic problems and meagre production.

Discussing the concept of self-interests, James Buchanan (1989) too points out that the individual has a better understanding of what gives satisfaction. Even though individual differences do exist, the pursuit of self-interests is common to all people. Buchanan argues that the impulsive pursuit of self-interests minus the many bureaucratic restrictions promote spontaneous order. Most people believe that they will succeed in enhancing the level of happiness and quality of life. Few people will be interested in pursuing their self-interests through the government. In Buchanan's views public choice can benefit tremendously from people having the freedom to pursue their own self-interests unhindered.

Undeniably, James Buchanan too fails to distinguish principle-cantered self-interests from selfishness. The pursuit of selfishness in the free market economic system has completely replaced the Smithian concept of principle-cantered self-interests pursuits. In modern times we are blatantly ignorant of Adam Smith's perspective on the relevance of moral principles and sentiments to the efficiency of the *laissez-faire* economic system. Unquestionably, we have also either explicitly or tacitly agreed with and have accepted the scholarly and business perspective that self-interested pursuits are tantamount to acting greedily in the free market economic system.

Scholars and business agents who view the relevance of the pursuits of self-interests to attitudes, behaviours, and actions illustrate a belief that the individual is inherently good. And since people are inherently good, when given the opportunity to pursue their own self-interests, they will act according to the dictates of the universal moral principles and benefit themselves and also indirectly bring net gains to others. The rational human being serving in the *laissez-faire* economic system will make decisions that will benefit the self and others indirectly. Viewed in this light the pursuit of personal self-interests is expected to enhance and sustain the wealth of nations. This perspective on the pursuit of self-interests is based on principle-centeredness. It underscores the belief that people are inherently good and that their pursuits of self-interests are principle-cantered.

However, when the assumption that people are inherently good does not hold any more, the pursuits of self-interests morph into those of selfishness. The implication of this reality is economically devastating to a people's wealth-creation and preservation process. In this situation the pursuit of selfishness leads to economic stagnation in the short-run and degradation in the long-run. The long-term outcome is recession and/or depression—depending on the degree to which severe human factor decay is prevalent among people in society. Only Adam Smith discusses the negative implications of the pursuit of selfishness to a people's economy (See Adam Smith, 1759). Unfortunately, since most people are unaware of Smith's book, *Theory of Moral Sentiments*, they are unfamiliar with this aspect of self-interest pursuits.

Robert Owen (1771-1858) and other scholars who pursued the socialist line of thinking challenged the classical view of the non-principle-cantered pursuits of self-interests. In an essay published in 1813 Robert Owen maintains that to achieve the greatest level of happiness, the individual must serve the community first. Owen argues that: "The happiness of self, clearly understood and uniformly practiced...can only be attained by conduct that must promote the happiness of the community" (Quoted in Brue, 1994, p. 177. See details in Robert Owen's book, *A New View of Society and Other Writings*. London: Dent, pp. 17-20). Other scholars who also elaborated on the concept of self-interests and its impact on a people's wealth-creation process include Sismode de Sismond and Karl Marx.

When community members follow their own self-interests to the detriment of others, their attitudes, behaviours and actions force the whole society into economic difficulties in the long-run. The personal desire to satisfy selfish self-interests in spite of the imminent negative effects it exerts on others, minimizes the degree of effectiveness of the *laissez-faire* economic system. Arguably, the personal lack of integrity leads to the corruption of self-interests pursuits. In this manner the pursuit of self-interests morphs into that of selfishness. The pursuits of personal greed and acts of fraudulence determine people's attitudes, behaviours, and actions in the free market economy. Market agents who suffer from the excessive drive of selfishness indulge themselves in acts of deceitfulness, mismanagement, misappropriation, and misapplication of funds.

Community members who are given to the pursuit of

unrestrained selfishness indulge themselves in acts of lawlessness and deception. They are prepared to engage in any kinds of attitudes, behaviours, and actions that bring to them financial gains regardless of the negative implications for all others. This practice of corrupted self-interests (i.e., selfishness) is indicative of how certain estate managers in ancient Greece managed other people's estates strictly with their own personal gains in mind. This kind of economic practice is what is referred to as *Chrematistike*.

These individuals are governed by the desire for acts of covetousness and the willingness to dispossess others out of their property in any way possible. These individuals shelter themselves from the sufferings of those they hurt through their acts of selfishness. The gains they derive through these acts of cruelty and dishonesty blind them to the suffering of those they dispossess. If the *laissez-faire* economic system is to work as efficiently as we desire and hope for, it must be based on the principles of *Oikonomia* and not Chrematistics. *Oikonomia* refers to economic practices that take into consideration principle-centeredness. It is about managing the estate to profit everyone. That is, the practice of *Oikonomia* mandates that the pursuits of self-interests be carried out on the basis of personal adherence to the dictates of the universal spiritual and moral principles.

Today, it is remarkable to observe that in western civilization the meaning of the word *economics* has increasingly become more and more synonymous with *Chrematistike*, while it continues progressively to lose its meaning of *Oikonomia*. Few business people today see themselves as being in business aimed at the careful management and maintenance as stewards on behalf of others. This reality has fuelled and promoted the pursuit of avid selfishness with the sole purpose of creating personal wealth on the back of others. Such a practice weakens the moral foundation of the efficiency of the free market economic system.

Adjibolosoo points out that real life evidence of the avid pursuits of selfishness is evident in the actions of professionals as well as amateurs in the various marketplaces in every economic system. Arguably, it was these people's pursuit of selfishness that pushed the global economy into the current long-term recession which began in 2007. Undeniably, therefore, the degree to which market agents pursue principle-cantered self-interests is dependent on the quality of the human factor.

The critical policy recommendation that emerges from this powerful empirical evidence is that free market efficiency requires leaders, subordinates, agents, and patriotic citizens who understand that the most important variable that propels or hinders economic growth and human-cantered development is the quality of the human factor. The true foundation of an excellently functioning free market economic system is the positive quality of the human factor. Until these qualities of the human factor are developed, deployed, and sustained, any attempts made to deal with economic recession and/or depression will fail. Currently academic theorizing undertaken in the discipline of economics and aimed at solving economic problems fails to take into account the critical role of the quality of the human factor in creating or solving the problems. We will return to a more detailed presentation on the significance of the quality of the human factor in Chapters 8, 9, 10, 11, and 12.

4

Key Assumptions of Orthodox Economic Theorizing

In this chapter, our main emphasis is placed solely on a selection of the key assumptions that lay the basic foundation for economic theorizing and their implications for the efficiency of the *laissez-faire* economic system. Though the list of assumptions presented in this chapter does not necessarily exhaust all assumptions evident in economic theorizing they are, however, representative of the key reasons why most *laissez-faire* economists argue against the intrusion of the draconian visible hand of government officials in the free enterprise economic system. To gain a deeper understanding of the significance of everyone of these assumptions and the degree to which they together reveal the free enterprisers' misunderstanding as to what actually makes the *laissez-faire* economic system to achieve its best outcomes is the first step along the path toward gaining deeper insights into our failed economic planning, policy making, project design, and program implementation (i.e., the 4 Ps Portfolios). Every time we fail to deal effectively with the economic problems that face us, it is because our unflinching trust in these assumptions together misleads us.

Arguably, therefore, the lack of a deeper understanding of the significance of the quality of the human factor is the primary source of the failure of modern economic theorizing and the prescriptions made for problem solving through the 4 Ps Portfolio. This lack of understanding is evident in certain key sweeping generalizations modern economists make in terms of that which makes possible the efficiency of the *laissez-faire* economist system. When these assumptions are strictly binding, the 4Ps Portfolios based on theoretical economic prescriptions have greater probabilities of working well. When these assumptions prove to be false, and they frequently do, economic theories and their attendant policy prescriptions about free markets miss the mark. What most economists are unaware of is the implicit assumptions made about the quality of the human factor in every presupposition they apply in economic theorizing. Arguably, contrary to the views of Milton Friedman (1953), assumptions do matter in economic theorizing. But Milton Friedman is not alone in this kind of thinking. Several other economists too take this same position. Paul Samuelson and William Vickery too believed and argued that excellence in economic theorizing depends on the consistency of the assumptions made use of rather than realism.

In an article he published on *The Gains from International Trade* in 1939, Paul Samuelson argues that "In pointing out the consequences of a set of abstract assumptions, one need not be committed unduly as to the relation between reality and these assumptions." The conclusions Samuelson drew from this paper have been falsified by real life empirical evidence present in the British and Germany experiences attained in industrial supremacy through their practice of protectionism.

Writing about the irrelevance of assumptions in economic theorizing, Vickery, a Nobel Laureate in economics in 1997 argues that:

Economic theory proper, indeed, is nothing more than a system of logical relations between certain sets of assumptions and the conclusions derived from them...The validity of a theory proper does not depend on the correspondence or lack of it between the assumptions of the theory or its conclusions and observations in the real world. A theory as an internally consistent system is valid if the conclusions follow logically from its premises, and the fact that neither the premises nor the conclusions correspond to reality may show that the theory is not very useful, but does not invalidate it. In any pure theory, all propositions are essentially tautological, in the sense that the results are implicit in the assumptions made.

Obviously, Vickery too failed to understand the true significance of assumptions to model building and theorizing in economics. He does not even think that either a set of prevailing or newly emerging empirical evidence matters as far as false assumptions are concerned. To him, even when key assumptions are not binding at all, Vickery believed that the model or theory is still valid. As long as a theoretician's assumptions make it possible for him or her to formulate any theories of choice there is no need to worry about the empirical falsification of the foundational key assumptions on which the model has been built. Wow! How most economic scholars have been misled for generations unending by the brilliance of the highly respected brains in the field! Certain economists have always believed and continue to argue that for as long as personal self-interests are served in economic model building there is no need to worry about whether or not the assumptions made are valid. The reader must bear it in mind that Friedman, Paul Samuelson, and William Vickery are all Nobel Laureates in Economics.

Viewed from the human factor perspective, the argument that assumptions do not matter is a cover up for intellectual ignorance. Professor Milton Friedman is, however, right when he notes that time is the best test of any theory and the validity of the assumptions on which it is formulated. These assumptions are unable to explain the diverse forms of market imperfections we experience in a cyclical manner. Undeniably herein lies the *Achilles Heel* of poor economic theorizing and its implications for policy ineffectiveness. In what follows we take a look at some of these presuppositions and what their assumed relevance is deemed to be.

Presuppositions of Orthodox Economic Theorizing

The foundation explicit as well as implicit presuppositions provide to economic theorizing determines the long-term validity and explanatory power of economic theories. The recommendations economists make provide the primary foundation on which the effectiveness of orthodox economic thinking, theorizing, and policy actions rest. Some of the most explicitly stated assumptions include the existence of relatively stable institutions, efficient financial institutions, sound work ethic and social ethos, unhindered pursuit of self-interests, the rationality of human behaviour, full information, and perfect foresight. The significance of each of these presuppositions is discussed in the following subsections.

Relatively Stable Institutions

The assumption that the effective functioning of free markets requires the existence of relatively stable institutions is foundational to classical as well as neoclassical economic theorizing. These institutions are expected to provide the appropriate ethos and corresponding regulations required to govern people's attitudes, behaviours, and actions. While some of these institutions may be subject to frequent changes, others are not.

Examples of those institutions that change frequently are those affected by laws. Laws such as anti-trust laws, tax laws, rent control laws, assigned property rights, and labour laws determine the welfare of these institutions. Aspects of the law are in the state of ongoing change because of lack of full information and perfect foresight when initially legislated! Also, those who are committed to violating the law are frequently one step ahead of those who enforce it. As a result, the agents of law enforcement often have to play catch-up with those who are bent on violating the law. To make matters worse, new amendments to existing laws to strengthen them take a considerable length of time to create and implement.

We are daily being forced to create new regulatory measures on case-by-case basis. With these new laws we expect to confront newly emerging challenges we didn't anticipate. In nation states the most stable institution is the people's primary governing document, *The Constitution*. These constitutions are relatively stable. They are a little harder to change than other aspects of the existing legal system. People debate all proposed amendments to their constitution. While some amendments are accepted, others are rejected. An excellent constitution, when honestly interpreted and applied, gives stability to the nation as a whole. With this stability and trust in its execution, the constitution brings good judgment, justice, equality, peace, and harmony to the citizens.

The existence and efficient functioning of each of these institutions is expected to provide the required environmental conditions for advancement. These propel the efficiency of free markets in the *laissez-faire* economic system. The social institutions, for example, are expected to provide the deterrence and stability required for free market efficiency. The social institutions include the: *Family, Government, Economy, Education, Law, and Religion* (Table 4.1).

Social institutions are tools humans have created and continue to create and evolve to deal with the numerous challenges and problems faced. They are used to meet the unlimited needs people have. Through these institutions, humans create and develop further over time diver frameworks applied to the satisfaction of the basic as well as the higher needs.

The functions of the basic social institutions are listed in Table 4.1. It is important to remember that each of these social institutions is a human creation. The economic institution on which we concentrate in this book is, for example, a human social institution created to deal with the economizing problem. In every society, the economic institution plays a central role in the people's life. Through it, people are able to generate financial resources with which they satisfy their basic needs. As human challenges balloon, many more systems and institutions are created and used to face the new challenges. Yet these new additions do not necessarily lead to the annihilation of any of the basic social institutions. At best, they add to their effectiveness.

Table 4.1: The Basic Social Institutions and their General Functions

Institution	Functions
Family	1. Control and regulation of sexual behaviour 2. Provision of new members of society (procreation) 3. Offer economic and emotional health and maintenance to members 4. Socialization of children, youth, and adult members
Government	1. Institutionalization of norms (Laws) 2. The enforcement of laws 3. Conflict adjudication (Court). 4. Provision of welfare to members of society 5. Protecting society from external threats 6. Organizing and providing political administration
Economy	1. Providing methods for producing goods and services 2. Creation and operation of methods for distributing goods and services 3. Enabling members of society to consume the goods and services 4. Seeing to the most efficient use of scarce resources
Education	1. Socialization 2. Education and training: Preparation for occupational roles 3. Transmission of culture 4. Evaluating and selecting competent individuals 5. Transmitting knowledge, skills, competences, and abilities

Contd...

Religion	1. Providing solutions for unexplained phenomena 2. Offering a means for understanding and controlling the natural world 3. Supports the normative structure of the society 4. Giving meaning for life and human experiences 5. Serves as an instrument of socialization 6. Promoting social change (or may also be retarding it) 7. Reducing and encourage conflict in groups (or promoting conflicts).
Law	1. Promoting and providing justice 2. Ensuring order and safety 3. Works for peace and tranquillity 4. Offers protection to all community members 5. Outlining and enforcing prohibitions 6. Imposition of sanctions on violators

Source: The data used to construct Table 4.1 is drawn from http://www.tomcravens.com/inst.html

In the worst case, these new developments may create inefficiencies to the existing practices in the basic social institutions.

Common knowledge has revealed that no single human being is perfect in the expression of attitudes, behaviours, and actions. To create the necessary checks and balances on the expression of unbridled free will, the social institutions are required to provide the requisite institutional arrangements to guide people to act appropriately (Table 4.1). The nature of sanctions imposed on violators is stated in detail in the law.

When necessary, the institutional arrangements put in place are used to regulate people in the expression of their attitudes, behaviours, and actions. As long as people engage in the expected attitudes, behaviours, and actions, they are left on their own to pursue their self-interests without any overbearing institutional limitations. Those who violate cherished institutional norms are apprehended and penalized. The reliability of effective legal and social institutions is indispensable to the efficient functioning of free markets in the *laissez-faire* economic system setting.

Efficient Financial Institutions

Classical and neoclassical economists maintain that the existence of efficient financial institutions is *sine qua non* to the appropriate functioning of the *laissez-faire* economic system and free market performance. A people in any community who lack these institutions are unable to provide adequate financial capital to support economic growth and sustained human-cantered development.

Efficient financial institutions are deemed to be invaluable in supporting entrepreneurial activities such as invention, innovation, effective leadership, efficient management, and the wealth creation process. The efficient functioning of these institutions is expected to ensure long-term economic prosperity in free market economies. The absence of efficacious financial institutions spells disaster to the local as well as national economies.

Sound Work Ethic and Social Ethos

The absence of a well-established system of sound work ethic is a treacherous enemy to high performance and market efficiency in the *laissez-faire* economic system. People who possess a well-organized system of sound work ethic are bulwarks of their society. They make free market economic activities work as efficiently as possible. They attain the objective of higher total factor productivity.

People with such work ethic maximize the use of their own scarce FEET resources. Such people avoid waste in the applications made of their FEET resources. They neither shirk nor indulge in the destructive act of absenteeism. A people's adherence to existing work ethic and social ethos provides the much-needed guidance in the pursuit of attitudes, behaviours, and actions. These ennoble and enable the wealth creation process in free markets.

Rational Behaviour: The Freedom to Pursue Self-Interests

Classical and neoclassical economists maintain that the pursuit of unbounded self-interests leads to the maximization of the wealth creation process. When left unfettered, as the argument goes, individuals pursue self-interests to the best of their ability. It is argued that these individuals directly promote their own gains. By so doing, self-interested pursuits indirectly foster the interests of other community members without intentionally intending to do so. These aspects of net benefits that accrue to others are the unintended positive outcomes of the expression of individual self-interests (see details in Chapter 3).

Undeniably, classical and neoclassical economic theorizing maintains the rationality of human behaviour. Economists of this persuasion assume that economic agents act in *reasonable* manners to facilitate their successes in achieving intended objectives of utility maximization by consumers or profit maximization by producers. Adam Smith (1776) maintains that the invisible hand leads each person to pursue personal self-interests without overtly affecting the needs and interests of others. According to Adam Smith, this individualized behaviour enhances the wealth creation process of nations.

Speaking to the Smithian concept of self-interest pursuits and the guidance the Invisible Hand provides, Blumberg notes that:

Most people have powerful impulses of self-interest and somewhat weaker impulses in altruism. That being so, social institutions can be designed to try to bring self-interest into harmony with public interest, so that the inevitable pursuit of self-interest will yield the common good. On the other hand, institutions can be arranged to set the powerful impulses of self-interest in direct conflict with public interest, so that the pursuit of self-interest will frequently produce anti-social behaviour.

A critical reading of Blumberg's (1989) sloppy and erroneous perspective quoted above will lead some naïve scholars to agree *in toto* with his insights. Viewed from the human factor perspective, Blumberg is dead wrong in his thinking. First, Blumberg is unaware that social institutions are inanimate. Second, due to their inanimate nature, Blumberg is unaware that social institutions take on the life and character of those who design, implement, manage, and lead them. Third, social institutions are only as good and effective as those who design, implement, lead, and manage them.

The redesign of these institutions will produce identical results as previously as long as the quality of the human factor has not been transformed for the better. For centuries humans have suffered from this same erroneous thinking and warped judgment. The undeniable truth is that the quality of the human factor is key to human successes and failures. We'll return to the development of the human factor concept later in the book and flesh it out.

Undeniably, the unhindered pursuit of self-interests in free markets, *ceteris paribus*, grows and sustains the wealth of nations. Yet it is also an undeniable fact that it is only under those conditions where the quality of the human factor improves that those who serve in these institutions enhance their productivity in the diverse marketplaces.

Perfect Foresight and Full Information

In classical economic thinking and theorizing Adam Smith (1723-1790) implicitly assumes that people are generally *inherently* good. Though not explicitly stated in his writing a critical analysis of Smith's philosophical perspectives on the functioning of the *laissez-faire* economic system reveals his belief in *the inherent goodness of humans*. In his book, *the Wealth of Nations*, Adam Smith writes: "By pursuing his own interest he frequently promotes that of the society more effectually than when he really intends to promote it...It is not from the benevolence of the butcher, the brewer, or the baker, that we expect our dinner, but from their regard for their own interest." *The Invisible Hand* is the mechanism that leads people to promote community welfare is the market system that functions via the forces of competition (i.e., demand and supply).

As a strong proponent of freedom, Adam Smith argues that the essence of the system of natural liberty prescribe that every individual must be left alone to pursue his or her own desired self-interests in beneficial ways as long as they do not violate the laws of justice. From the Smithian perspective, this practice could enhance, propel, and secure the wealth of nations.

Neoclassical economists presuppose that economic agents operating in free market economies possess full information and always make good decisions. As the argument goes, access to full information in addition to the set of existing fixed rules guides people to pursue the goals of utility as well as profit maximization with few limitations. It is only in those cases when full information doesn't exist that actors in free markets face conditions of imperfect information and uncertainty. These people integrate new information into their decision-making processes and choices when it becomes available to them.

Observations

When the *explicit* as well as *implicit* assumptions are in full force, policies based on classical and neoclassical economic theorizing promote and sustain stable social interaction, organization, and productivity. This outcome promotes the virtuous performance of people who serve as the custodians of the social institutions and free markets in the *laissez-faire* economic system.

These presuppositions are powerful and relevant. What most economic theorists and free market proponents are unaware of is that their validity depends on the quality of the human factor. Generally, classical and neoclassical economists have tacitly argued that the quality of the human factor is always positive. This is the primary source of their confidence in the predictive power of their theories and the effectiveness of the *laissez-faire* economic system. What they are unaware of is that for any of these critical presuppositions to be biding, the environmental conditions must exude a blend of the qualities of the human factor that tips more on the positive side than the negative. That is, the communities where the qualities of the positive human factor trump those of the negative.

Even in the cases of an excellent balance (i.e., a balanced blend) of the positive and negative human factor qualities prevails there exists a greater likelihood that the free market economic system will perform rather well. Sadly, though, in most real life situation in communities, the expressions of the negative qualities of the human factor trounce those of the positive. Arguably the blend of the expressions of the qualities of the positive and negative human factor matter significantly in terms of the efficiency of the free market economic system.

5

Genesis of Economic Problems and the New Challenges

For approximately three centuries, from the 1500s to the 1800s, Mercantilists controlled the use of labour and capital resources in England. The candour and astuteness of these Mercantilists during this period of time in human history catapulted the British into leadership in the then known world. They created the resources required to explore and conquer the world. The voyages and expeditions of discovery they financed assured the British naval superiority over other competing nations. British Mercantilists felt economic policy must be aimed at the creation of a national economy whose sole purpose was to enrich the then British Crown (Ruggiero, 1927).

The policies and practices of the mercantilists redirected attention to the encouragement of production and exportation. The *English Navigational Acts* reveal that adherents of Mercantilism favoured exports and restricted imports. International trade was generally one way and based on the idea of selling to others without purchasing anything from them using gold and any other precious metals. The sole objective of Mercantilist trade policy was to acquire and stockpile gold and other precious metals to enrich and strengthen the British Crown.

The English Mercantilist concept and the practice of its restrictive economic and commercial policies engendered acute revulsion in certain French scholars referred to as the Physiocrats (Skinner, 1937; Soule, 1937; and Spender, 1937). The philosophical underpinning concept of Physiocracy, *Natural Liberty*, is the belief that every human being must be free to pursue personal self-interests, exert labour, and enjoy the fruits of industriousness as long as his or her own private actions do not violate the rights and freedoms of others (Robertson, 1925; Laski, 1936; Mill, 1947; and Rosenberg, 1979).

As a direct result of the underlying philosophy of Physiocracy, the desire for economic individualism led people to demand freedom from the rules and regulations imposed on them by mercantilist government officials. Through the intense exercise of the power of mind and reason, liberalism was catapulted into life and became a powerful force that has sustained *laissez faire* economic practices into modern times (Filler, 1939 and Croce, 1941).

Viewing the concept of wealth creation and improved human welfare from this perspective, the Physiocrats argue that there is the need to create a *Social Order* and a *Political Economy of Development* within which every human being is free to pursue self-interests without any draconian government intrusion and limitations (Hobson, 1909; Hobhouse, 1911; Hollander, 1925; and Hoover, 1934). The process of national wealth creation must focus primarily on the attainment of the gamut of individual freedoms, equity, good judgment, and justice for all (Wasserman, 1944, pp. 27-30).

This is the kind of economic liberalism Adam Smith describes poignantly in his classic book, *An Inquiry into the Nature and Causes of the Wealth of Nations*, first published in 1776. Scholars of *History of Economic Thought* have noted that when Adam Smith visited France, he had extensive dialogues with Francois Quesnay (1694-1774), the founder and leader of the *Physiocratic School of Thought*. The discussions Adam Smith had with Quesnay and his colleagues on the physiocratic idea of *natural liberty* impressed him so much that he incorporated them into his own discussions and teachings on the underlying philosophy of *classical liberal economics* at his own home *school of classical economic thought*. At this school, Adam Smith promoted the concepts of free trade and markets, individual natural liberty, the pursuit of self-interests, fairness, and justice for all people in society. Adam Smith's belief in natural harmony led him to conclude that economic laws, when allowed to operate freely through demand and supply forces, will lead to maximum productivity and optimal wealth creation in society.

Challenges We Face: Recession and Our Action Steps
Corporate America as well as the economic world in other developed countries is on fire! But this fire is not the kind that burns and consumes houses and trees. It is fire that is representative of fraudulence, accounting scandals, and various types of corruption in business practices and economic activities. In the last several years, numerous Chief Executive Officers (CEOs) and Chief Financial Officers (CFOs) forced companies like Enron, Arthur Anderson, Global Crossings, and many others into bankruptcy. As the facts have revealed to date, most of these CEOs and CFOs earned their academic degrees from Ivy League business schools in the country. While engaged in the study of courses aimed at completing the necessary requirements for their degrees, these individuals were required to take either a course or two in business ethic. By having been exposed to the contents of the required ethic course(s), the general assumption is that students are prepared and equipped with adequate ethical knowledge to deal with ethical dilemmas and moral questions that arise at the workplace in the various marketplaces.

However, when graduates get employed, they realize that the knowledge kit they bring along with them is insufficient for dealing with the moral questions and ethical dilemmas they are confronted with. Though they are most frequently adept in the intensity of ethical knowledge and can articulate well the moral question, they most frequently fail to make morally right and ethically sound decisions. Clearly, forcing students to take one or two required courses in ethics does not help that much in minimizing scandals in business, education, politics, and social life after all. Graduates are, therefore, unable to deal appropriately with the ethical problems and moral dilemmas they are exposed to.

Today we are once again at a critical watershed of the continuing unfolding of human history. Recent global economic phenomena with ubiquitous business bankruptcies and the failure of the leaders and managers of giant corporations as well as the disappearances of these once mega financial enterprises have revealed that we are more vulnerable to the worsening of the quality of our attitudes, behaviours, and actions. Sadly we seem to not have the power to control and redirect our energies that drive these attitudes, behaviours, and actions.

The current recession seems to have taken us by surprise and we are struggling to play catch up. Renowned economists, highly respected business gurus, politicians, social activists, lobbyists, and consultants of diverse persuasions, though ignorant about the actual root cause of the current recession, continue to lay audacious claims to their knowledge of the precise answers to the problem.

As usual, there are numerous conferences, consulting sessions, newspaper briefs, academic position papers, radio and television infotainments, and talk shows aimed at minimizing people's fears and nipping the feelings of paranoia in its bud. Speeches of political leaders flow like furious desert streams that aren't only in a hurry, but also bent on sweeping away deadly matter that blocks their path of progress. Government leaders, managers, and administrators from all over the world continue to think, believe, and issue memoranda to the effect that they can tax and spend themselves out of the complex economic problems that beset us today.

Yet, it is sad to note that the shallow thinking on the part of everyone involved in the solution process will only bankrupt every one of us as long as leadership ignorance reigns. Unless we wake up to the true knowledge and understanding of the root cause of today's economic problems, we will end up exacerbating the degree of severity of the economic problem and the new challenges it brings. Most people are neither aware of this reality nor feel the complexity and strength of its winds of change. Either our combined knowledge will guide us to emerge victorious or the thick layers of ignorance we experience will make us the big losers. To transcend the plight of the destruction that originates from our spiritual ignorance and moral failings, we must choose our lifestyles wisely. Above all, we must commit to intentionally walk the path of principle-centeredness. Now is the most appropriate time we must reflect critically on the significance of the confluence of the political economy of the quality of the human factor and our avid desire for the expression of liberty, self-interests, civility, and social justice. The functioning of the free market economic system and the implications for individual freedom and the strength of our endurance to sustain the wealth-creation process will be guaranteed by the improvements we make to the quality of our human factor.

New Economic Challenges of Our Times
There are numerous problems in the global Macro economy today. If a company or an industry is struggling to survive, it means only one of two things: The company or industry is not doing well financially or it has already reached the point of bankruptcy! When smaller companies are experiencing tough times, they rarely receive financial stimulus packages from leaders of government. They are not bailed out. These companies' owners are left to find their own financial solutions. They are exposed to the whims of free market forces. The manner in which these forces function makes the ultimate decision for the struggling companies as to whether to fold or continue on with their operations.

Contrariwise, when a large company is experiencing operational or survival challenges, cries come from citizens and political leaders to do something to prop them up.

Historical evidence reveals that government leaders implement stimulus packages today as they did during the great depression. Subsequent but milder recessions of the 1970s, 1980s, and 1990s were dealt with in a similar fashion. The accumulated empirical evidence since the great depression of the 1930s confirms that John Maynard Keynes' ideas are neither truly dead nor irrelevant to economic policy formulation and implementation today! He is alive in our hearts. His tall spirit of macroeconomic knowledge, understanding, and wisdom towers tall over us. His ghost is so encompassing to such a degree that we are unable to thoroughly evaluate and rethink his strategies for the 1930s and 1940s! Maybe this is good news for us in disguise. We must be thankful to him for his ever perennial but voiceless presence. Alternatively, this too may signify bad news for all humanity. Viewed in this light, one of the most challenging questions is: Where do we go from here and what must we do to alter the decrepit state of the economic conditions we face today?

The challenges are the impressive presence of John Maynard Keynes and our never-ceasing consultations with him in absentia are both a blessing and a curse. It is a blessing because we are able to tap into his wisdom and apply any advice to our situation without having to do any intimidating heavy lifting—thinking twice! Contrariwise, it is a curse because when we consult with the ghost of John Maynard Keynes, the whisperings we think we hear from his ever silent insinuations and recommendations are whole-heartedly accepted and implemented. Few intellectuals and government leaders involved in the problem solving process seek to know the precise source of the economic challenges we face today.

When such redemptive economic actions are taken with the sole purpose of lending a helping hand to the market forces by assisting particular companies or industries, little is known about the true causes of the problems being experienced. We seem to ignore the similarities between our economic challenges today and those of the era of John Maynard Keynes. No wonder we are eager to consult with him blindly rather than do a little more critical thinking for ourselves. We prefer to piggyback on his ideas regardless of whether they are still relevant to us today. We are both unprepared and unwilling to think deeply to find more appropriate solutions for the economic challenges of our day. Undeniably this is the Achilles' heel of our perennial economic theorizing and policy-making.

Knowledge of the Precise Source of a Problem

It is true that until the precise source of a problem is known, there can never be any long-term effective solution to it. The mere resurrection of certain ideas of our long-departed immediate family members, friends, colleagues, and ideology academicians, ideologues of our academic disciplines may not save us from the throes of economic recession/depression! Solutions drummed up from the misconceptions of the knowledge of the long-departed and applied to our problems most frequently turn out to be quick-fix ventures and problem-accommodating measures. These attempts aimed at dealing with the problems on hand are seldom potent long-term answers to pertinent problems. These quick-fix solutions and problem-accommodating measures fail to achieve our expected outcomes. They ignore the real root causes of the primary problems we face in the company or industry. At best, they are nothing more than glorified smokescreens and problem accommodation techniques.

The types of the solutions being proposed for dealing with the stagnation of the American as well as the rest of the global economy today may produce certain short-term results. The economic challenges of today include the real estate or housing market bubble in the USA and elsewhere, the personal financial (debt) crises, the financial meltdown, and the near-death experience of the banking industry. Diverse reasons are given to explain the housing bubble in the United States.

Included among these reasons are: the American mania for home ownership, belief that housing is a good investment, media promotions, speculative fever, purchasing and merchandizing houses far above normal multiples, the crash of the dot-com bubble, low interest rates, risky mortgage products, and lax lending standards.

Unfortunately, though, the real foundational cause of the emergence of these factors is most frequently left out and neither discussed in detail nor unaccounted for officially. However, certain newspaper and certain magazine articles have hinted at and discussed the degree to which greed and deception have contributed to the collapse of the housing market in the United States. Arguably, people's desire to get rich quick at the expense of others through acts of excessive fraudulence rooted in selfish and greedy practices is the sole perpetrator of the collapse of the housing market in the United States. These practices are results of *severe human factor decay*. In the long-term the kinds of solutions being pursued and implemented may never achieve our intended objective of solving the problem in the housing market. Until the proper corrections are made to the artificially overblown values of houses at most locations in the country, the housing glut will remain for many years to come. Someone will have to assume the losses in one form or the other. Without these become realities in the housing market, the proposed solutions we continue to call for and implement will fail to deal effectively with the primary root cause of the problems we face in the house as well as the stock market. Undeniably, the quality of the human factor is sine qua non to the efficiency of any market.

Since the First World War the United States has experienced tremendous increases in its gross domestic product (GDP). Yet within this same time period it has experienced these forms of economic downturns: recessions and depressions. The current downturn became obvious by the 4th quarter of 2008. Almost everyone was aware that we had already entered into a period of debilitating recession. We had never before experienced this unique kind of recession. Regardless of what government leaders did in 2008 through· their forceful injections of trillions of taxpayer dollars into the US economy, it has become unquestionably apparent that such an effort may not necessarily lead Americans out of the recession any time soon. Regardless of the short-term gains we may experience and boast of, we will experience more severe downturns in the long-term. In the spring of 2010 the severe economic haemorrhaging of certain European nations such as Greece has heightened fears that the current recession is not yet over as we are being prompted to believe.

There is countless number of Americans today discouraged and worried about what may happen to their accumulated wealth, retirement savings, quality of life and the education funds for their children. Many US citizens have lost all or significant proportions of their savings and accumulated investments. Others have lost their pension funds. The financial and the real estate markets as well as the retail sector have been hard hit by the current recession. Americans and people from other developed nation states are experiencing higher levels of unemployment, panhandling, prostitution, abject poverty, pet neglect and/or abandonment, homelessness, spousal separation, divorce, and spousal/child abuse.

The lack of a deeper understanding of what brought us to where we are today has produced fly-by-night intellectual counsellors and consultants of diverse disciplinary persuasions. Self-styled expert consultants and financial gurus are who we all flock and look to for the most comforting answers to the current economic as well as financial market problems. They provide economic guesses that are only as good as anybody else's. What most people are ignorant about is the true source of the current economic debacle in the United States. Arguably, you can't solve a problem when you are ignorant about what its real root cause is. When this is the reality for any people, the easy solution is to fall back on previously failed policy prescriptions.

In the long-term we perceive to our utter dismay that these solutions aren't as potent as we had previously been cajoled to believe. Albert Einstein is right when he notes that the problems of today have been created by yesterday's thinking. If we desire to solve today's problems with yesterday's thinking, we will be in deep trouble! Worst of all, Einstein and many others have pointed out that insanity is doing things the same way over and over again and yet expecting a different result. Yet when we become stuck, we revert to failed attempts of the past through our consultation with the ghosts of those intellectuals whose ideas aren't relevant today. The long-term impact of this practice is our perennial failure to break the back of the problems that face us.

The foregoing presentations and reflections bring to light a series of critical questions. Key among these queries include:

1. What are the current solutions being touted and pursued?
2. Are they working with the long-term in mind or not?
3. Will they work in the short-term?
4. What must we be doing today to succeed in dealing with these problems in the short-term as well as the long-term?
5. Are there key issues that are not being addressed?
6. What is the true source of strength and key foundation of free market efficiency?
7. Have global, national, regional, and community leaders ever worked collaboratively to establish and continually strengthen this foundation in the foregoing years?

To avert our unpleasant experience of recessions/depressions, we must become aware that there exists a strong interconnectedness between the quality of the human factor on one hand and the expression of personal liberty, avid self-interests, the nature of civility, and the quality of the kind of social justice spawned. Today, everything we have done to date in the attempt to deal with the recession has bypassed the only solution we must employ to deal with its true root cause, *severe human factor decay*. We have either failed to acknowledge or rejected the human factor dimension of the current recession. To guide us back to the kinds of solutions we must pursue in our attempt to deal with this recession, diverse arguments are made to reflect the true interconnectedness among these concepts and how our total neglect of the most appropriate programs will decimate our true capacity to create and sustain wealth in the long-term.

The emphasis in this book is placed on how to guide leaders and citizens in the developed and developing countries to use free market-based policies to improve the people's quality of life in the arena of the social institutions. While we become fully consumed by what we do in each of these areas, we must never lose sight of the primary source of the challenges that bedevil us in every sphere of life.

The principle of natural liberty requires that every individual be free to engage in any attitudes, behaviours, and actions as long as no one is harmed or limited in rights, freedoms, and privileges. Unfortunately the significance of this concept to free market forces is not well understood by the majority of leaders, professionals, academicians, and a whole host of other audiences. Worst of all the awareness of this concept is missing in the expression of attitudes, behaviours, and actions of the inhabitants of the developed and the developing countries. Having taught Principles of Economics internationally for many years, I am aware that even undergraduate students with academically promising brilliance and leadership qualities find it too difficult to comprehend the physiocratic idea of natural liberty and Adam Smith's (1723-1790) concept of *self-interest* and their relevance to *classical economic liberalism* (see details in Chapter 2).

What is even much more difficult for these students, intellectuals, and academicians of all philosophical persuasions to understand is how belief in self-interests propels attitudes, behaviours, and actions in the free market economy (Anshen, 1940; and Hayek, 1944 and 1945). Most professors as well as students of modern economics fail to gain a deeper understanding of what each of these free market ideals is and how they relate to the notion of *laissez-faire* economics and free market efficiency. This failure is, however, not the doing of any of these students per se. Instead, it is a result of the failure of their high school teachers and college professors to guide them to discover the truth about that which propels the *laissez-faire* economic system. These teachers and professors are themselves so lost in the thick forests of philosophical or ideological battlegrounds that are not able to provide the proper guidance their students require to discover the truth about the human factor foundation of free market efficiency for themselves. *Quel Dommage!*

Yet by failing to comprehend how these concepts work in synchronicity to initiate and expand the wealth creation process in the *laissez-faire* economic system, students as well as their professors, business leaders, and government administrators fail to grasp the significance of the pivotal idea of *the freedom to choose* (Friedman and Friedman, 1980) The core of this kind of freedom is about the personal decision to engage in productive income-generating activities; exert labour power; create and exchange value; and to acquire and dispose of personal property (Friedman, 1962; Friedman and Friedman, 1980).

6

Sources of Inaction and Failure

In light of the discussions presented in the foregoing Chapters 4 and 5, it is appropriate to ask the following additional questions:
1. Why have these foundational issues of economic modelling and/or theorizing been ignored for centuries?
2. Why are disciplinary scholars afraid of writing and/or speaking about these misconceptions and the problems they birth?
3. Why do brilliant economists commit to prop up and substantiate the key tenets of wrong philosophical and ideological perspectives?
4. Has these pursuits of self-interests gone so awry that by so doing blinded certain economists to the human factor foundation of the tenets of the kind of classical economics as Adam Smith spelled them out in 1759 and 1776?

The precise answers to each of these key questions neither require advanced knowledge in rocket science nor doctoral degrees in complex mathematical lemmas and statistical analysis. Why cannot most of our political administrators and their academically brilliant economic advisors perceive that the answers to these queries are nothing more than commonsense thinking? For most government officials and their associated economic advisors, the lack of deeper thinking is embedded in the ideology of self-preservation through the pursuits of non-principle-cantered self-interests. For other scholars and political party adherents and members, the paralyzing fear that grabs and wraps tightly around them renders them helpless. They become like Egyptian Mummies incarcerated in centuries of a cocoon woven with party ideologies as well as disciplinary perspectives. In what follows, we discuss this issue in detail.

Finding the Courage to Critique

Wisdom embedded in a traditional Ewe proverb from Ghana in West Africa provides the counsel that it is unwise to speak rudely and in anger to any members of the crocodile family to remind them of their long and ugly snouts. For example, if you are committed with any mode of premeditation to speak this unwelcome truth to members of the crocodile family, you must first have successfully crossed the crocodile-infested body of water to the intended shore of the ocean. After having done so, you've earned the right, the freedom, and the courage to express this sentiment to every member of the crocodile family. The worst damage they can do to you is to snarl their long and ugly snouts at and breathe empty threats at you!

In academia, this wisdom is both a protective covering and an excellent counsel to prospective neophytes in the field. At the beginning of their publishing careers young academic scholars must tread carefully the territorial waters of philosophical and ideological perspectives. Playing by the rules brings safety and a long productive academic career and life. Playing against these rules may mean instant or a painfully slow death! The only exception to this rule is to have the courage to speak out and be ready to do battle with the chief crocodile as one plunges into the water in an attempt to walk or swim across the river.

It is undeniable that those who have been crowned with the highest honour in their disciplinary fields have earned the right to critique the core tenets of the academic discipline in which they have received the highest honour. For without having crossed such hurdles ahead of time, it is foolishness to mount an extensive critique of the works of the leaders and gatekeepers of the field. It is for this reason that most scholars are usually silent and never intentionally rock the academic boat and by so doing jeopardize its intended course and acclaimed intellectual and underlying philosophical position. These individuals ensure that the academic traditions and philosophical positions reign. Thus the doyens remain on the throne of the reigning philosophical perspective. If we challenge the renowned gurus of the classical doctrines of any academic discipline we dig our own intellectual graves.

I remember quite fondly and vividly the time I began to work on my PhD dissertation in econometrics. During the research period, I discovered some well-known and highly regarded proposition coined by one of the top scholars in this field. Let us name him TJ. I discovered that one of his propositions about a certain critical issue in Bayesian Econometric Analysis wasn't quite accurate. When I reported this to one of my supervisors, his immediate response to me was in the following manner: "You're just beginning work on your PhD Dissertation in this field. You're a neophyte. What makes you think that you are more brilliant than TJ, one of the most intelligent scholars in this area of the field of econometrics?" Without any arguing with my supervisor, I brought the material to him to peruse. After he had reviewed the material, he agreed that I was right and TJ, the genius, was wrong. We worked on a scholarly journal article and had it published without any difficulties! Truly, even dogs can eat of the crumbs that fall off the edges of their masters' tables. Undeniably, we only fail when we neither take the initial steps nor try.

Disciplinary wisdom, a sacred cow to the doyens of the field, is not fair game for young and naïvely bourgeoning academicians who are still in their infant years of academic advancement and are still wearing intellectual diapers in the discipline. This is how most aspiring PhD candidates are forced to remain loyal to nonsensical ideological perspectives or concepts that do not make any sense at all in diverse academic disciplines. To want to do so about the works of seasoned and renowned scholars in the discipline implies the dangerous risk of not being able to complete the dissertation requirement for the earning and conferring on you the highly coveted doctor of philosophy degree. Worst of all, you may end up losing excellent career opportunities in either academia or elsewhere of significant personal interest. The graveyard for this group of scholars is filled with both ABDs (i.e., all but dissertation) and those who failed their thesis requirement for earning the degree.

The move to slander the doyens of the field and/or slaughter their ideologically sacred cows is one of the worst deeds an emerging brilliant scholar can attempt. Such an act of academic heroism is tantamount to the commission of an intellectual academic suicide. That is, to engage in academic treason is to have hanged oneself. Those who do so without having been already honoured with their degrees and/or a Nobel Prize in the discipline and all the privileges that come with these recognitions in their specific fields will never be patted on the back and blessed with the offer of the highest accolades of the Academy. To be labelled an outsider to mainstream thinking in a discipline is to be forced into its peripheries to forage on intellectual crumbs. Those who fall into this category have no chance at all of the opportunity to attain the highest possible honour in the discipline—earning the Nobel Prize—a most highly coveted laurel!

This reality is what brings ideological stagnation and disciplinary irrelevance to an academic discipline. Certainly areas in some disciplines or even whole disciplines have suffered this plight. Those who rebelled are eternally banished or deemed to be either *persona non grata* or deemed to be non-existent or have slipped into academic obscurity or disrepute! Throughout the centuries of our beleaguered history on Planet Earth few scholars have taken the risk of ostracism and presented powerful critiques of their disciplinary traditions that are fuelled to the brim with flaws in their foundational assumptions and thinking.

By reading, reviewing, and critically reflecting on diverse critiques of economic theorizing and policy in the last two centuries, it is not obvious why certain scholars did dabble in such critiques. A more thorough reflection, however, gives up the primary reason for such boldness on the part of each of these scholars from other disciplines at certain points in their academic careers.

Galileo Galilei (15 February 1564–8 January 1642) championed and supported the heliocentric view in opposition to the geocentric view. According to the philosophers of the geocentric view, the Earth is at the centre of the universe. Galileo from around 1610 disputed this view and began to publicly support the heliocentric view that the Sun is at the centre of the universe. By so doing, he put his whole life on a momentary hold. Then it later plunged into chaos and hopelessness. He was bitterly opposed and denounced by most philosophers, astronomers, and the leaders of the Catholic Church. He found himself at the mercies of the leaders and members of the Roman Inquisition in 1615. The leaders of the Catholic Church at that time denounced Galileo and condemned his perspective on heliocentrism. In February 1616 Galileo's perspective was deemed to be contrary to the biblical Scriptures. He was forced to abandon his perspective and he did temporarily.

Hearing clearly and listening attentively to the audible voice of personal principle-cantered self-interests, Galileo was convinced that he was right. He risked his whole life and career and stood up for and defended the truth he had discovered. He didn't yield to the powers that be. Initially, these powers seemed to have succeeded in opposing and oppressing him. But he later retracted and defended his perspective in his work, *Dialogue Concerning the Two Chief World Systems* in 1632. Galileo was accused of heresy, tried, found guilty, and forced to recant. He was arrested and placed under house arrest for the remainder of his life: from 1634 to 1642 (http://en.wikipedia.org/wiki/Galileo_Galilei).

There are some exceptions to the rule. The expression of academic brilliance in certain cases did not attract the kinds and levels of persecution that Galileo was subjected to. In these cases, those who challenged the existing views could articulate effectively the new perspectives they have gained access to. They did so in such a manner that the existing and reigning theories and their proponents could do nothing else to admit defeat and retreat. For example, when Newtonian physics emerged from the brilliance of Isaac Newton (1642-1727), few people had anything else to say against it. Similarly, when Albert Einstein (1879-1955) showed up with quantum physics, few of his contemporaries had anything else to say! However, when Mahatma Gandhi (October 2, 1869-January 30, 1948) rose up and challenged the status quo regarding certain immoral human dealings, he paid for his actions with his life. So also did Dr. Martin Luther King, Jr. (January 15, 1929-April 4, 1968). For Nelson Mandela (July 18, 1918), it was a whopping twenty-seven years in solitary confinement on Robben Island! Today, the Republic of South Africa is a nation we all adore. By standing by his own pursuits of principle-cantered self-interests, he brought hope to all humanity.

Karl Marx (1818-1883) did not have it easy, regardless of his academic brilliance. Recall, for example, when he critiqued capitalism, he was at a point in his life when he had absolutely nothing to lose. Yet he suffered dire consequences that transcended his lifetime. For having challenged reigning intellectually revered ideas, and powerful tool of wealth acquisition, he became a man without a job, home, family, nation, and emotional satisfaction. Literally, he became a fugitive without any permanent country. His whole life was filled to the brim with indescribable misery all through to the time of his demise.

The Plight of Disciplinary Critics in the Academy

King (1988) has compiled a list of economists he daubed the *Economic Exiles*. The only crime these economists committed was taking a stand against the weaknesses they observed to be inherent in orthodox economic thinking and theorizing. Among this list of Economic Exiles are: Sir James Steuart (1713-1780), Edward Stillingfleet Cayley (1802-1862), John Francis Bray (1809-1897), Henry George (1839-1897), J. A. Hobson (1858-1940), Major C. H. Douglas (1879-1952), Paul A. Baran (1910-1964), P. W. S. Andrews (1914-1971), and E. F. Schumacher (1911-1977). The only crime each of these scholars committed was to question mainstream economic thinking and propose alternative paths to improving upon the quality and relevance of economics as an academic discipline. They are heretics and deviants regarding their perspectives on mainstream economic thinking. The powerful and combined voices of these scholars neither counts nor respected in any way.

Mocking these scholars and their contributions, John Maynard Keynes (1971, pp. 193-194) observes:

The heretic is an honest intellectualist, who has the pluck to stick to his conclusions, even when they are surprising, so long as the line of thought by which he reaches them has not been refuted to his own understanding. When, as in this case, his surprising conclusions are also of such a kind that, if they were true, they would resolve many of the economic ills of suffering humanity, a moral enthusiasm exalts and strengthens his obstinacy. He follows, like Socrates, with unbowed head wherever the argument leads him. He deserves respect; and it must be the duty of anyone who writes on this subject to make the attempt to clear the matter up and to reconcile heretics and bankers in a common understanding [Quoted in King, 1988, p.1].

Note that John Maynard Keynes first mocks these scholars and then recommends that others should give them the benefit of the doubt. Undeniably, scholarship in the Academy is requires that members to follow the laid down traditions. To transgress the boundaries is to become a heretic. Regardless of your academic brilliance and the deep well of wisdom gained through lifetime experiences, you are no more than a heretic and/or deviant of science in the Academy you have loved and cherished. The nagging question as to why the critical and vocal scholars of the Academy are labelled as heretics and summarily excommunicated has been poignantly answered. Writing about this issue, King (1988, pp. 1-2) notes:

If successive generations of economists have been guided by a single basic theory which they have refined and extended over centuries to yield more and more information about the working of the economy, then the rejection of dissidents can be seen as a necessary condition for scientific advance, a welcome process of replacing error by truth. If, on the other hand, the history of economics is one of continual and continuing conflict over concepts and frameworks of analysis; if the belief in increasing economic knowledge is itself contentious, and there is disagreement over the very criteria of what is to count as 'known'; then it may be dangerous to neglect the contributions of heretics and theoretical outcasts in the name of intellectual progress."

As King (1988) has pointed out precisely, the majority view is the former. The latter perspective is unacceptable to many in the Academy. Yet Thomas Kuhn (1962) has argued convincingly that during any scientific revolution, there emerges a redefinition in that while some problems become more predominant of greater concern, others are classified as being uninteresting and/or unscientific.

Most frequently, though, the scholars who propose that which is sometimes misunderstood and wrongly labelled as uninteresting and/or unscientific perspectives are lambasted and either forcefully expelled out of the Academy or totally ignored. This practice is actually unscientific. With this perspective in mind, Ludwig Von Mises (1949, p. 5) is dead wrong when he observes that "The physicist does not mind if somebody stigmatizes his theories as bourgeois, Western or Jewish; in the same way the economist should ignore detraction and slander. He should let the dogs bark and pay no heed to their yelping. It is seemly for him to remember."

These kinds of treatment are aimed at either silencing them officially or ignoring and hoping that they will fizzle away unnoticed. Truly, when two elephants fight, it is the grass that suffers. One wonders about the place of relevance to dealing effectively with the economizing problem as the elephants in the Academy fight it out. Unfortunately, they have led to poor modelling and economic theorizing. Those economists who believe in these kinds of recommendations most frequently bury their heads in the sand and pretend that more one else except they only know how economic theorizing must be carried out.

What a pitiful position to adopt in a discipline that so desperately needs help to advance!

When John Maynard Keynes (1883-1946) engineered Keynesianism, the whole world was experiencing severe depression and people from everywhere were looking for a way out. At that time most people were open to any recommended solution that would work. Confident that he was right and could convince others to go along with his ideas, John Maynard Keynes took the sword of his academic intellect and with it slashed open and disembowelled Say's Law of Markets. After having done so successfully, he paraded the casket of Say's Law of Markets and displayed it in the funeral home erected in the minds of the chief doyens of the field of Macroeconomics.

The empirical evidence he employed at the time was overwhelmingly obvious and undeniably damning. He was fortunate that his ideas worked at the time. He escaped the ordeal of academic trial by the fire of burning hatred and perennial ostracism. He went on to become a highly decorated and celebrated hero! Today, he still has numerous admirers as well as enemies. The macroeconomic ideas of John Maynard Keynes still reign supreme. Arguably, the personal possession of a clear and accurate thinking mind, a loving and passionate heart, and the sword of personal courage do lead to great achievements that lead all humanity on to new and oceans and horizons that could not have been discovered in any other ways. There, they do battle and lose their shackles of fear, suffering, and hopelessness. Without this calibre of people we remain in our stupor eternally as beaten up humans.

It probably makes little sense to either ignore or critique any form of academic scholarship without having even understood its primary thrust and significance in the first place. For example, was John Maynard Keynes wrong when he opened the door for the visible hand of government officials to step in to deal with the challenges posed to the efficiency of the *laissez-faire* economic system by the prevailing currents of the Great Depression in the 1930s? Why didn't the free market forces correct themselves immediately after the crash in 1929? How much time did the market forces require to bounce back by on their own into doing what they did best in the past? Why did it take the efforts of the visible hand officials to bring some welcome changes and good news to people during that moment in time?

These, I suppose, are a billion dollar questions that still today require thoughtful scholarship to respond to with great brilliance. Unfortunately, though, to just dismiss John Maynard Keynes' effort at the time as being a great failure is to include one's self among the academically unwise scholars of the times. To avoid this label, be prepared and readily willing to hear the questions first. Take some time to reflect more deeply upon their primary thrust and then respond wisely rather than intelligently to them. In this manner, you will avoid the label of being an unwise scholar in the Academy. Arguably, though, those who have zero knowledge as to the depth of the Keynesian perspective at that time will do well to keep their mouths shut and fountain pens locked up in their penholders and wisely stashed away from sight so they may not be misused.

The Dark Side of the Pursuit of Non-Principle-Centeredness

There is, however, a dark and sombre side to the pursuit of personal self-interests and ideologies that are non-principle-cantered. Take, for example, the case of Adolf Hitler (1889-1945). When he rose up with his concept of Nazism, most Germans were ready to climb on board because of fear and also for the purpose of self-preservation. His tactics of intimidation, assassination, and ostracism worked well for him. He won the hearts of most Germans and took the whole world out for a deadly ride. The fear of death was so paralyzing that few people dared to challenge Hitler and his henchmen who were deadly killers. The timid and fearful Germans were coerced and lured into accepting by the ideology of Nazism. The end result was human wickedness unclothed in broad daylight. Hitler and his team were deadly!

Few people can challenge the status quo and emerge unscathed. Few people have the courage to point out that the emperor is naked! For this reason, sloppy ideologies, worldviews, and concepts remain in circulation for decades—if not centuries. The primary reason for this reality is the fear of losing one's place among the respected scholars and ideologues of the field. This behaviour is also good for self-preservation and sustenance. This behaviour preserved certain poorly conceived ideological perspectives for too long in our world. The cost to us has been untold long-term human untold suffering for centuries. In economic theorizing it hasn't been all that easy to critique traditional concepts. Yet, with great courage, wisdom, and tact, Adam Smith (1723-1790) dethroned the Mercantilist philosophy of economics and business.

Yet, today, to rise up against economic classicism is to shut the doors to one's potential for winning the Nobel Prize in the discipline of economics. To covet this prize is to have made a covenant with oneself to fall in line and place a permanent lid and padlock on one's lips, thinking capacities, and writing abilities! The only exception to this rule relates to those who have already been honoured with the Nobel Prize. For these honourees it is possible to voice out a critique of the classical doctrines of economics and still keep one's earned honour in the field. But this does not imply that others will not slander you in other diverse ways.

Professor Paul Krugman Take on the Academy

Take, for example, the September 2009 critique of classical economic doctrines by Professor Paul Krugman. For decades Professor Paul Krugman had written books, academic articles, and newspaper columns on diverse economic theories and policies. In September 2009 he published a critique of some key assumptions and the manner in which economics has become mathematicized in *The New York Times*. It is understandable that Professor Paul Krugman could voice out his views regarding the weaknesses inherent in orthodox economic theorizing.

Professor Paul Krugman could remind the members of the crocodile family, to which he somehow belongs, that they possess long and ugly snots. He probably had already successfully crossed the academic river which is filled with deadly crocodiles. Not much can hurt him now in terms of his personal academic as well as professional career.

Yet, regardless of his heroism, two things strike an intelligent reader of Professor Paul Krugman's critique of modern economic theorizing. First, there is little in his critique that is new. What Professor Paul Krugman has adduced as being his damaging critique of economic theory is common knowledge. He runs no potential risk of being left behind or dishonoured at all! Writing about his frustrations regarding what he deems to be the failure of modern economic theory, Professor Paul Krugman inveighs the assumptions and policy recommendations that emerge from traditional economic theorizing. What Professor Paul Krugman may not have been aware of is that hundreds of scholars have, with excellent passion and relentless candour, made similar critiques in the past. Sadly, though, Professor Paul Krugman never alluded to any of the leading authors of the perennial insightful critiques of economic presuppositions and theories in the past (see a listing in Adjibolosoo, 1995, 1999; See also Thorstein Bunde Veblen, July 30, 1857-August 3, 1929 and John R. Commons, October 13, 1862-11 May 1945).

Secondly, it is not exactly clear what sets apart his suggested recommendations for improving modern economic theorizing and policy making from all others. With this observation in mind, the human factor theorist wants to know about how different Professor Paul Krugman's proposed solutions are from the existing ones. To what degree does Professor Krugman's proposed solutions differ from current theorizing in financial economics from which he draws his recommendations? Professor Krugman, by propounding a solution that is positioned in the theory of financial economics, reveals that he too has absolutely no clue about the *Achilles Heel* of modern economic theorizing and policy.

The Mathematicization of Economic Theories

Regardless of these observations regarding Professor Paul Krugman's critique of modern economics, I do share his critique of the insane mathematicization of the subject. Undeniably, economics is a moral science. The intentionality of the leaders of the Academy to make it a mathematical science has by now ruined diverse aspects of the discipline—especially its normative roots. Members of certain groups of economic theoreticians do gloss over the reality that a great deal of economic information cannot be easily captured in a mathematical model. I fully agree with Screpanti and Zamabi (1993, pp. 8-9) in their view that:

We wish, however, to avoid falling into certain 'mesological' naïvities and simplifications, which often contribute to the production of histories of economic thought by portraits, or treating the evolution of ideas as an appendix to the evolution of economic facts. We realize that the reality studied by the economist is not fixed like that of the natural sciences. Economic facts change through time and space: problems which appear crucial in a certain period may be irrelevant in another, and those that are considered important in one country can be completely ignored in another.

This peculiarity of the subject of investigation may help to explain part of the history of economic thought, for instance, the existence of certain national peculiarities or the emergence of specific theories at certain historical moments...There is no doubt that the cultural background and the 'visions' of the scientists have a strong effect on their research activities; and still more determinants are the common ideas and values accepted by the scientific communities, as it is precisely these which select and give direction to the individuals. But more generally, there is no doubt that it is the particular society as a whole which determines the cultural climate in which the choices available to individual scientists and scientific community are provided and delimited. Society as a whole decrees the importance of the problems to be studied, establishes the directions in which solutions should be sought, and, ultimately, decides which theories are correct.

Emerging from the foregoing quotation is the undeniable fact that economics is strongly rooted in the customs and traditions of a people. As such the people's habitual practices, though not necessarily measurable, play a central role in their pursuit of economic/business activities.

This reality mandates that to be successful in building relevant economic models economic theorizing must integrate the cultural dimension of a people's live. This task can be easily accomplished through a better understanding and integration of the quality of the human factor in economic theorizing. This is the way to go in that the only thing that is common to members of diverse cultural groups is the centrality of the quality of the of people's human factor. This is the primary reason why human factor theorists argue that a better understanding of the quality of the human factor will lead to more effective and relevant economic theorizing across diverse cultures.

In their current state, most economic theories have little relevance to our own comprehension of the normative aspects of economics and what we must learn from them to thoroughly educate ourselves in terms of how to tackle the economic/business problems that face us daily.

Much of modern economic theorizing is nothing more than intelligently thought out and sculpturing of convoluted ideas through the applications of mathematical knowledge. There is little substance to this practice of mathematical economic modelling because it misses the point of fostering a better understanding of principle-cantered self-interests that play a major role in the efficiency of an unhindered *laissez-faire* economic system. For mathematical economists, economic model building is nothing more than the applications of quantitative methods for the purposes of impressing peers, colleagues, and foes about their personal wealth of knowledge and the ability to apply them to economic theorizing.

While sculpturing in the pure arts is often displayed lavishly for the general public to observe and appreciate, this is not the case of mathematical economic modelling. Though mathematical economic modelling is aimed at dealing with everyday economic problems, it is not pursued with the intent of being displayed in theatres for the general public to appreciate. This is true because these models are not designed to guide planning, policy formulation, project design, and/or program implementation.

Instead, the mathematical sculpturing of economic models differs from artistic carvings in that economic theories are first presented to economists during departmental seminars or annual academic conferences patronized solely by economists. Secondly, since most of these carved mathematical models can neither be appreciated as a fine art work nor understood by the non-trained mathematical economists, they live and die naturally on the pages of academic journals or in electronic file folders. In most cases their applications in the developing countries, their primary testing grounds, have left trails of untold human suffering and pain: hunger, starvation, disease, and death. Plans, policies, projects, and programs based on models of mathematical economics have led to the worsening of the quality of life in these nation states. Worst of all, the sole patrons of these models are ignorant government officials (i.e., the visible hand of government) who, though illiterate in economic thinking and analysis, seek such models to validate the imprudent decision they have already committed to pursue by unduly regulating the *laissez-faire* economic system.

Classical economics emerged during the tail end of the Eighteenth Century. As such, its core was deeply rooted in the eighteenth century Scottish Enlightenment Era. Its primary ideological underpinnings included such concepts as moral philosophy—the pursuits of principle-cantered self-interests (not selfishness), *laissez-faire*, natural liberty, love for self, respect for others, and the belief in the existence of an *Impartial Spectator* who guides people to contemplate the individualized attitudes, behaviours, or actions prior to engaging in them. The expression of any person's attitude, behaviour or action in the *laissez-faire* economic system is modified by that which Adam Smith referred to as the *Invisible Hand*. The Impartial Spectator is nothing more than the progenitors of personal feelings regarding what one's responses must be regarding the outward expressions of attitudes, behaviours, and actions.

The Impartial Spectator is the prompter of a person's own awareness as well as speculations of the nature of the responses of other community members in relation to his or her actions in the marketplace. The personal speculations regarding what other people's responses to the expressions of unique attitudes, behaviours, and actions serve as *a social thermometer* to judge the degree to which the indulgence in certain behaviours will be accepted and rewarded or rejected and punished.

Knowing and acting correctly on one's feelings ensures positive responses in the form of applauses. However, if one misjudges or intentionally goes against the required social ethos, the responses are swiftly shown in the expressions of condemnation and calls for immediate punishment or long-term banishment or ostracism. Clearly, when a person's attitudes, behaviours, and actions are in line with the expected responses of others, the individual's Impartial Spectator is externally induced. The individual's expectation of the degree of severity of social sanctions for having violated customary norms is the sole determining factor in deciding to engage in any decision or abandon it.

Arguably people whose lifestyle choices are based on external rewards or sanctions depend on the guidance provided by the external Impartial Spectator. These people's moral development is tantamount to what Lawrence Kohlberg (1958) referred to as the first stage of moral development. Drawing on the work of Jean Piaget (1932), Kohlberg (1958, 1971, and 1981) argues that a person's moral reasoning, the foundation for ethical behaviour, passes through six stages of development. Each subsequent stage reveals a higher capability of the individual to engage in deeper moral reasoning and sounder ethical decision making in relation to more complex moral dilemmas. In his work Kohlberg showed that the process of moral development is essentially concerned with justice (see also Kohlberg, Levine, and Hewer, 1983). This development process is carried out throughout the whole lifespan.

Viewed from Kohlberg's perspective of moral development, the nature of attitudes, behaviours, and actions one engages in are propelled by the belief that no one else will know about or discuss these wrongful acts. It is this belief that encourages the individual to engage in wrongful attitudes, behaviours, and actions. Arguably, the personal feeling of secrecy and the high likelihood of not being apprehended for having engaged in any morally reprehensible acts reinforce the desire and willingness to violate moral principles in order to attain one's intended mission. Members of this group of people frequently pursue self-interests that are non-principle-centered.

However, people whose Impartial Spectator is embedded within their core of inner being and triggered by internally induced obedience to the dictates of the universal principles are those who have moved on to higher levels of Kohlberg's stages of moral development. The Impartial Spectator works in them through their principle-cantered conscience rather than external rewards and social sanctions. Members of this class of people are better-positioned to make the *laissez-faire* economic system work to attain its optimal outcomes. This is because these people's self-interested pursuits are principle-cantered. The ebb and flow of economic activities in any *laissez-faire* economic system is a product of which of these two groups of players' attitudes, behaviours, and actions dominate transactions in the free market economic system.

Unfortunately the modern economist is unaware of these realities and has refused to delve deeper into the foundational moral principles that underscore the efficiency of the *laissez-faire* economic system. In a fast-tracked attempt to exorcize the moral foundation and the principles on which its effectiveness is assured modern economists have, with little understanding of the actual thrust of classical economics, elected to force a moral science (i.e., economics) into becoming a discipline of pure science. In their pursuit of this objective they have with great premeditation tossed out the moral foundation of economics.

Though this outcome is thrilling to mathematical economists and lovers of mathematics who may have sought refuge in economics it is a great loss to all humanity. This is the case because the modern scientific method and its tools do not deal with the moral principles they can neither measure nor experience through the five senses. By so doing mathematical economists have ruined the discipline. Instead of calling their new body of academic knowledge something else and claiming its fatherhood they prefer to cruise on Adam Smith's academic brilliance and reputation. After having done so in mathematically intelligent manner modern economists proceed to assert that neither economic principles nor markets have any morality embedded in them. This conclusion too is an untenable assertion on their part.

Oh how wrong they are in their claims! Their assertion is so ludicrous that even a first year economics student would laugh at them for their failure to understand that Adam's Smith's first book, *The Theory of Moral Sentiments*, describes in no uncertain terms the moral foundations of an efficient free market economic system. By recklessly expunging the moral principles and annihilating them as the foundation of modern economics they have birthed, they have made it impossible for others to have a better understanding of the proper focus of the Smithian economics. Sadly, though, even their success in the mathematicization of modern economics has not made modern economic theorizing an effective tool for solving everyday economic problems.

The mathematical approaches to the study and analysis of economic phenomena lead to no useful outcomes outside the conferring of a Nobel Prize on those who can doodle mathematically. The move to make economics a discipline that was originally rooted in moral philosophy into a pure science has led to the discarding of its most influential normative root, *the moral principles in which it was originally positioned.* What this action has done to the discipline is bankrupt it of its reliance on practical economic issues and how to deal with them effectively. The race to render economics an objective scientific discipline has defrauded its practitioners of the understanding of its normative underpinnings. We have gone off on a tangent and are now unable to fully understand the economic challenges we face or how to deal with them effectively.

When we are faced with such challenges in the form of recessions and depressions, we commit our scarce FEET resources toward bankrupted swimming sessions in spheres of life where our accumulated numerical data banks do not serve as sources of the problem. We never discover the solutions to our prevailing economic problems in these places. Yet even in our failures, we refuse to search for authentic answers to the normative domain where the real solutions dwell and beckon us to discover them. To understand these realities, we must become more familiar with the primary reasons why mathematical economists cannot understand the Smithian perspectives on the pursuit of principle-cantered self-interests.

The glorification of mathematical analyses in economic science and the demonization of its moral foundations have together made people convinced that economics is a dismal science and has little to offer toward dealing with the economic and business challenges we have faced for centuries. Worst of all, this failure has denied modern economists the opportunity to become familiar with and gain a better understanding of the relevance of the quality of the human factor to the efficiency of the free market economic system.

These realities evident in the practice of modern economics explain in detail why some of these mathematical economic theoreticians, though not having ever read Adam Smith's, *The Theory of Moral Sentiments*, give lectures and speeches across the nation and declaring to their friendly audiences that "Greed is good. Greed makes you feel rich and happy." And of course, they are not ashamed to lie to their unassuming audiences that they wrongly and unjustifiably quote Adam Smith to prop up a non-principle-cantered perspective they have. *Quell Dommage!*

As to the question: "How did economists get it so wrong?" The answer is now pretty obvious. That is: modern economists are unenlightened about the truth that classical economic analysis is positioned in moral philosophy rather than in the applications of the methods and tools of pure science. Mathematical economists have got it so wrong because they, with great premeditation, have refused to allow the principles of moral philosophy to define their academic as well as professional scholarship in economic theorizing. They failed to understand the significance of the quality of the human factor to the efficient functioning of the *laissez-faire* economic system. Until they return to the moral roots and foundation of classical economics, they will never succeed in making potent recommendations to government officials and free market agents to deal effectively with the economic challenges of our times.

Isn't it about time modern economists move away from the practice of squandering their time resources on bashing Karl Marx, John Maynard Keynes, and any others like these scholars about whether or not they were wrong in their theorizing and recommendations and begin a search more diligently for solutions that can work well for us today?

It seems to me that the only thing these economists know how to do best is to make economic policy recommendations that lead to the misapplication of our scarce FEET resources. The practice of channelling these scarce FEET resources into mathematical modelling is also a waste. We can do better than this. We can easily return to that which we rejected and make modern economics more relevant to our lives. We must go back and comb more diligently through Adam Smith (1759). After having done so with great assiduity, we will come into face-to-face contact with the undeniable truth that authentic economic modelling must be securely rooted in the quality of a people's spiritual capital and moral capital.

Undeniably lifestyle choices formed by virtuous living are *sine qua non* to free market efficiency. The quality of the human factor is intricately intertwined with the efficiency of the free market economic system. For without this knowledge, understanding, and the willingness as well as the readiness to apply it to modern economic theorizing, our craze for mathematical economic model building and its applications will lead us far off course and into dangerous territories of hot water where hard-earned wealth is destroyed.

By squandering almost all of their scarce FEET resources on the building of mathematical models, most economists seldom have what it takes to gain a better understanding of the primary variable (i.e., the quality of the human factor) that is the most effective foundation for the efficiency of the *laissez-faire* economic system.

These economists are, therefore, unable to guide government officials or even the average citizen to become more familiar with the economic challenges we face and how we must deal with them. Decades of teaching abstract economic models to undergraduate and graduate students have not yet changed people's views of economics as *the dismal science*. And rightly so! Economists have never been successful in assisting non-economists to gain a better understanding of the relevance of the subject as a problem-solving discipline. What a shame this reality is!

To conclude this chapter, it is important to know that real life experiences from the developed as well as the developing world confirm that modern economic theorizing hardly ever leads to effective problem solving in economics. An excellent example can be drawn from the experiences of Muhammad Yunus. He obtained his Ph.D. degree in economics from Vanderbilt University (USA) in Economic Development in 1971. Between 1969 and 1972 he began work on the concepts of micro credit and microfinance. It was during this period of time in his career when he learned that traditional economic theory was of no value to the poor people in the village. He founded the Grameen Bank and used it to provide help and also bring hope to the poor.

As noted earlier, economic systems are human creations aimed at dealing with the economizing problem. What most people are unaware of is that economic systems are inanimate. To successfully achieve their intended objectives and policy goals they require the qualities of the positive human factor of community members to function and remain functional as desired over time. In view of this, Gardner's (1998, p.17) view that: "The economic performance of a country is determined by its economic system and environment, and by the policies of its leaders," is not accurate. In the presence of continuing human factor decay and/or underdevelopment economic systems and their accompanying plans, policies, projects, and programs fail. Economic systems are human creations aimed at efficiently dealing with the economizing or scarcity problem.

The lack of this knowledge on the part of those who engage in economic theorizing makes it impossible for most of them to recognize and become aware that economic systems are inanimate. As such, they have no life of their own. The quality of life they have is infused into them through the animation of the people who are charged with the task of running, managing, and evaluating them. As such, to successfully achieve their intended objectives and policy goals every economic system requires the positive human factor qualities of community members to function and remain functional as desired over time. In communities where people who possess the positive human factor qualities are nonexistent, plans must be put in place to create education programs that well produce this calibre of people.

These realities reveal beyond any reasonable doubt that there is room for development planning in every country—developing as well as the developed nation states. Arguably, therefore, the massive practice of economic development planning in countries reveal the inherent humanly created weaknesses prevalent in the *laissez-faire* economic system. Yet contemporary development planning itself faces tremendous challenges posed by severe human factor decay.

Evidence confirming the failure of economic theorizing in its traditional form is overwhelming. Economists will never be successful in proposing solutions that work without having integrated the quality of the human factor in their economic modelling. The quality of the human factor is the most primary factor that determines the degree to which the free market economic system attains its efficiency. Without the availability of the positive qualities of the human factor, it is impossible for the laissez-faire economic system to attain its best outcomes.

Viewed in this light the synopsis written on Ludwig Von Mises' (1949) book entitled: *Human Action: A Treatise on Economics* is right on. In this summary, the author notes that "When the capacities and limitations of economic are ignored or misunderstood, the result has been less than misery and slavery for millions in an age that could have abundance with freedom and work."

Yet it is crucial to become aware that the misery, disease, hunger, starvation, and suffering we continue to experience in the world are not necessarily outcomes of statism, socialism, and totalitarianism as Ludwig Von Mises (1881-1973), Henry Hazlitt (1894-1993), and a countless number of laissez-faire proponents claim (see also Henry Hazlitt, 1988). These problems are common to capitalist states as well as socialist countries. Those who make these kinds of claims fail to understand that the real source of every one of these challenges is severe human factor decay.

7

Critical Reflections and Observations on Economic Performance

Bearing in mind our discussions up to this point it is imperative to ask a crucial question: "Whose voice should we listen more attentively to and whose must we ignore in the Academy?" Clearly the answer to this question depends significantly on what our objectives are for engaging in any aspects of our discipline. First, it is crucial that every member's voice be heard, discussed, and debated. To not do so is to behave both naively and with the thickest possible blinders on. Second, if our primary answer to this key question is to merely advance economics as a discipline of pure science without any concerns for whether or not our theorizing leads to the discovery of solutions that work in making the *laissez-faire* economic system deliver more efficient outcomes in our attempts to deal with the prevailing economic challenges that face us, then the answer is pretty obvious. Third, if, however, we are more interested in finding precise answers to that which lays the unshakable foundation for the efficiency of the *laissez-faire* economic system then we must look for answers that deliver this result to us as a sure possibility.

Undeniably, to date we have failed to be aware of each of these three distinct choices. As a result, we go off tangent and practice our discipline in ways that are more inhibiting rather than propelling. With this in mind, may be the time is now when we must engage in deeper and wiser dialogues amongst us as we search for that which informs the efficiency of the free market economic system. As we do so, we must become more mindful of the real reasons why economics exists as an academic discipline. To work hand-in-hand toward this objective will advance the discipline much farther than could be achieved in any other manners.

With these perspectives and the content of the foregoing presentation in mind, it is apparent that we must become more open to engaging in more thorough and insightful analyses of diverse critiques of economic theory and policy. We may sooner or later become more familiar with which types of critiques to take more seriously and which ones we may not have to for as long as they may not lead us toward the attainment of our primary objectives. Indeed, we may not have to pay any attention to critical views that are found to be mere reactionary gestures. Any pursuit of these kinds of recommended solutions will neither work nor point us in the direction of more promising reformulations of a badly ailing economic theory.

Worst of all, when accepted and pursued, recommendations that are bankrupt of the moral underpinnings of economics will lead us through the same old and stale intellectually empty alleys and back on to the barren paths we've travelled in the past. The pursuit of mathematical theorizing that ignores the significance of the quality of the human factor will unfortunately point us toward that behavioural world of failed economic theorizing, policy formulation, project design, and program implementation. Should we choose to pursue suggested directions of change that neglect the quality of the human factor, we will remain in the world of economic degradation and decay.

Such recommendations, like those of their predecessors with identical thrusts, are nothing more than new false starts. The end results of our pursuits that ignore the moral foundation of economics will be more damaging than the existing bad practices of economic theorizing we intend to ameliorate. The thrust of his critique demonstrates that most modern economists are not aware of the *foundation and core* of the failure of economic theorizing and policy making in the last one and a half centuries.

Anyone who desires to succeed in achieving and sustaining the efficiency of modern economics must possess knowledge about the hidden moral laws of efficiency in the *laissez-faire* economic system. These scholars must first understand what underscores the foundation and operation of the *laissez-faire* economic system. However, since this knowledge is lacking in orthodox economic thinking and theorizing, it is impossible that most recommended solutions will work as their authors and proponents anticipate.

It is unproductive for any interested reformers of orthodox economic theories to follow the same paths and utilizing the same kind of thinking that has led us to where we are today. Viewed in this light, I am not as optimistic as most modern mathematical economists. There is a place for quantitative analysis in modern economics. Arguably, though, I am convinced that we are yet to discover and make the best use of it. Given the paucity of our combined knowledge of what actually makes an economic system work it isn't clear to anyone how the restatement of previously failed solutions will work today. Where the requisite knowledge is lacking, little may be achieved through sporadic and grossly uncoordinated trial-and-error responses to seasonal or cyclical economic problems.

Undeniably, members of any group of people who don't know the precise source of their problems can not argue successfully about what constitutes an authentic solution. Writing to express the deadly nature of ignorance and its high costs to any group of people in their own communities in his book, *War and Peace*, Tolstoy notes cleverly but sadly that:

Doctors came to see Natasha, both separately and in consultation. They said a great deal in French, German and in Latin. They criticized one another, and prescribed the most diverse remedies for all the diseases they were familiar with. But it never occurred to one of them to make the simple reflection that they could not understand the disease from which Natasha was suffering, as no single disease can be fully understood in a living person; for every living person has his complaints unknown to medicine—not a disease of the lungs, of the kidneys, of the skin, of the heart, and so on, as described in medical books, but a disease that consists of one out of the innumerable combinations of ailments of those organs (Quoted in Jameson and Wilber, 1979, p. 35).

The thrust of the foregoing quotation illustrates perfectly the condition of those who are currently working to deal with the global economic challenges we had faced in the past and currently experience while suffering the experience of tremendous losses of wealth. Evidently, such recessions occur in a perennially cyclical manner because we do not know precisely what their root cause is. For this lack of knowledge our pet solutions have always concentrated on quick-fixes and problem-accommodation measures.

For no less than two centuries intellectually brilliant economists armed with their varied ideological perspectives like swords of war, developed theories and techniques aimed at diagnosing, explaining, conquering, and remedying economic problems. In these attempts renowned modern economic theorists have made generalized diagnoses and prescribed corresponding policies with which to transcend the problems that throttle the process of capital accumulation, economic progress, and the wealth creation process. Although these economic theorists focus their attention on the same problems, their resulting diagnoses and policy prescriptions are frequently at variance with each other. We end with our backs to the wall. The problems become entrenched. We wake up the next day only to realize that though our economic spaceship has been hit hard by the meteorite of severe human factor decay, we are still unaware of what hit us. To our utter surprise the problems don't only laugh at us with scorn, but become more complicated to deal with. They never go away! The badly marred economic spaceship continues to trudge on helplessly without any bearings. Arguably, our plight is akin to that of Humpty Dumpty:

Humpty Dumpty sat on a wall
Humpty Dumpty had a great fall
All the king's horses and all the king's men
Couldn't put Humpty together again

(Opie and P. Opie, 1951, pp. 213-215).

This simple nursery rhyme, rich and deep in unadulterated ancient wisdom, is loaded with excellent lessons and explanations for our perennial failures. Unfortunately, most of these explanations for our failures are hidden from the intellectual brilliance of the modern intelligentsias! Our intelligence and academic pride fail us. It is, therefore, not all that surprising that we continue to miss the excellent opportunities we are presented with daily to discover the true root causes of the challenges we have faced throughout the centuries. We just revel in our ignorance and the accolades it blesses us with. *Quel dommage*!

Since most of these policies derived from our past have been unsuccessful, we continue to remain like Natasha. We experience the misfortune of not being healed of the aggressive cancer that continually devastates our flesh. This is simply because our economic physicians, like the doctors of poor Natasha, are unable to agree on the causes and cures for our economic ailments. Our kings, queens, and their horsemen and other troupe members cannot help us at all. They have neither understanding nor solutions that will work anyway. As revealed through the plight of Natasha, when medical doctors act in ignorance and on guesses only, the likelihood that they will succeed is limited.

Every medical doctor involved in the healing process must acquire the knowledge about what ails the patient before the patient can be healed. Similarly, Humpty Dumpty remains badly wounded, hurting and with numerous broken bones. There is no one who can revive and restore him back to health to his honourable position at the palace. This outcome frequently produces sensations of failure, impotence, and hopelessness. If only we will be a little more willing to venture out into certain unexplored horizons without giving up, we may find the solutions to our problems today.

The truth of remaining in a state of helplessness and acting in ignorance is vividly illustrated in the story of this fly a colleague told me several years ago. He recalled that when he was once on vacation in Paris, France, he woke up one quiet afternoon from his siesta to an irritating and buzzing sound in his hotel room. As he followed the direction of the sound with his ears and eyes, he saw a furious and disoriented housefly searching blindly for an exit out of the hotel room. This fly struggled hard to fly out of the room to freedom! Its main strategy for escape to freedom was to thoughtlessly take off at great speed only to bang its head again and again against the glass walls! As if it were so this fly would voicelessly say to my friend: "Ouch, it hurts! Can't you please help me get out of this horrible jail room?"

Frustrated that my friend neither cared nor was concerned about its plight and desire for freedom, it would gather momentous speed and fly like a rocket right back into another part of the glass wall. As that fly continued on with this painful routine my friend attempted fruitlessly to redirect it to the doorway. The more he tried, the more his concocted rescue attempt failed. The discouraged and badly weakened fly couldn't fly toward the open door. For some reason, it was too afraid of this opening and never flew toward it. During the period of its ordeal it avoided the doorway in the manner dogs avoid fleas!

After numerous failed attempts, the fly got so tired that it fell onto the floor. It was at this point that my friend gently placed a piece of newspaper beneath, lifted it up, and gently walked it on tippy toe toward the doorway. As soon as this dazed fly began to feel the refreshing and soothing breeze, it spread its wings and took off at the speed of a loose cannonball to freedom! It was obvious that when this fly smelled and breathed in the fresh air, it exploited the opportunity to be free, took it, and regained its freedom! Undeniably, insanity is doing things the same way over and over again expecting a different result.

This observation portrays a reality. If a community of people is to derive any concrete benefits from the activities of orthodox economic theorizing and policy making, these theoreticians must identify what the foundation to sustained economic growth and development is. They must also know what the main hindrances to economic welfare are. Except when fully incapacitated, it is the patient who must tell the physician what he or she feels in the ailing body. This communication removes the necessity of having to engage in dangerous trial-and-error diagnostic procedures. This practice does complicate the severity of the economic disease.

However, when the patient describes symptoms that don't relate to the evidence of the actual disease, rookie doctors are often misled. They misapply their knowledge of treatment. Similarly, when the patient's accurate description of the signals of the disease is ignored, the recommendations the doctor makes lead to wrong treatment. These medical doctor's failures are mirrored in the inability of economists to recognize and exploit the underlying natural laws of economic growth and development.

One of the greatest dangers of mounting human ignorance is that it misleads us to believe in bankrupted solutions. The human pursuit of these kinds of attitudes, behaviours, and actions is tantamount to the perennial practice of flogging dead horses. The act of flogging a dead horse, a darling policy measure for ignorant leaders, deranged social activists, and their accomplices is reflective of:

Buying a bigger whip

Appointing a committee to study the horse

Arranging a visit to other sites to see how they ride dead horses

Increasing the standards for riding dead horses

Appointing a group to revive the dead horse

Creating a training session to improve riding skills on a dead horse

Changing the requirements so that the horse no longer meets the standard of dead

Hiring a consultant to show how a dead horse can be

ridden

Harnessing several dead horses together to increase speed
Increasing funding to improve the horse's performance
Declaring that no horse is too dead to beat
Doing a study to see if outsourcing will reduce
the cost of riding a dead horse
Buying a computer program to enhance dead horse
performance
Declaring a dead horse less costly than a live one
Promoting the dead horse to a supervisory position
(http://alistair.accountsupport.com/index.php/Riding_a_de
ad_horse).

Wow! Oh how we have got ourselves lost and barricaded
in a thick fog of ignorance and helplessness. We just cannot
find our way out of the maze of failures, helplessness, and
hopelessness. The journey to the hidden exit door is elusive
and traumatizing. Perennially, we are unable to reach it.

And regardless of how successful a people may be in
schooling their citizens, a countless number of others will still
be left out of existing opportunities. This reality is a result of
factiously sleazy discriminatory practices that separate
members of each of these two classes of people. In certain
cases those who are deemed to not be members of the
dominant and ruling or affluent class find it hard to transcend
the limitations conventional human practices in the social
institutions place on them in the labour market.

The kinds of discriminatory practices members of minority
groups are subjected to are reflected in race, gender, creed,
ethnicity, lifestyle choices, physical characteristics, and
wealth. And for as long as these labels exist, it is impossible
for members of minority groups to dwell within the walls of
good judgment and experience social justice. Since these
labels are encrypted in the core of inner being of the
perpetrators of social injustice, it is arguable that until people
are exposed to a curriculum of the transformational
development education program, the practice of gruelling acts

of social injustice will remain strong and in perpetuity (see Adjibolosoo, 1996a).

To transcend the challenging problems we face in the functioning of the laissez-faire economic system, we must become familiar with the key assumptions that underscore its theorizing and policy effectiveness. This knowledge will open our minds to that which we must do to transcend the petty economics challenges we face today. We now turn to the presentation and thorough analysis of this issue in the next chapter.

8

Quality of the Human Factor and Efficiency of Economic Systems

Evident in the Smithian perspectives on the pursuit of self-interests within the confines of natural liberty is that the performance optimality of the *laissez-faire* economic system relies solely on the strength and exercise of the positive qualities of each individual's human factor. Return to Chapter 1 and briefly review the definition for the human factor. Succinctly stated, the human factor is the array of personality characteristics that enable people to function effectively or do poorly in their roles in the social institutions. These social institutions are the family, government, law, economy, schools, and religion. What determines the degree to which the quality of the human factor impacts a person's performance in each of these social institutions is whether or not that individual's human factor quality leans more heavily on the positive or negative side of who the person really is?

The quality of the human factor is as pertinent to economic performance as the central nervous system is to the efficient functioning of the human body (see Adjibolosoo, 1995a, pp. 3-30; Kasliwal, 1995, pp. 3-24; Cypher and Dietz, 1997, pp. 3-53; and Todaro, 1997, pp. 3-18). The degree to which the quality of the human factor is developed or underdeveloped in every person affects the effectiveness with which the individual functions in a free market economic system.

While the development of the positive human factor enhances input productivity and economic progress, its decay leads to the degeneration of the effectiveness of the economy and other social institutions (Adjibolosoo, 1996a and 1996b). Indeed, from the human factor perspective, the quality of attitudes, behaviours, and actions are invaluable to economic growth and human-cantered development (Adjibolosoo, 1994, 1995a, 1995b, and 1995c). Every human being using the acquired human factor qualities is capable of propelling the economy's efficient performance.

To be optimally efficient, we must engage in each of these activities within the confines of natural liberty (Hallgren, 1941). To achieve this objective, we must produce relevant reading materials on the primary role of the human factor for a beginners' course in liberal studies for the high school and college students. Using these materials, these students will be assisted to attain deeper levels of understanding of the significance of the quality of the human factor and its implications for the attainment of natural liberty and the sweet pursuit of self-interests. This is exactly the primary task of this book. The reading material produced and presented in this book aims at promoting and ensuring students' understanding and embrace of the philosophical underpinnings of classical economic liberalism. The primary premise of this book is the possibility of discovering procedures rooted in the quality of the human factor that enable agents in free markets to attain and sustain the path that leads to the optimal wealth creation process.

The contents of this book highlight Adam Smith's views regarding the *laissez faire* economic system. The presentations made in this book explicate the significance of the quality of the human factor, *the nature of personality characteristics*, to the principle-cantered pursuit of self-interests. It is concluded that without having developed positive human factor in ourselves, it is impossible for our attitudes, behaviours, and actions to propel free market forces to achieve the highest possible level of efficiency attainable in the *laissez-faire* economic system.

Our task today as advocates of classical liberal economics is to ensure that the fire of classical economic liberalism is never extinguished anywhere in the world. For this reason it is our duty to educate the leaders of the next generation and opponents—if there are any out there, especially in the developing countries, to uphold the flag of classical economic liberalism and keep its lamp of individual freedom and self-interest pursuits burning and glowing brighter.

Yet at the moment we are failing to achieve this objective. To transcend this failure, we must engage in relevant scholarly activities that will ensure that the members of next generation of academicians in the developing as well as the advanced countries understands the significance of the quality of the human factor to self-interest pursuits and its relevance to the efficiency of free markets. It is this understanding that will encourage them to work with us to pursue and preserve free market principles.

The rise of the social democrats and the strength and audacity with which they take us back to the era of BIG governments, BIG labour, and BIG Business is an excellent reflection of the fact that the free enterprisers are themselves grossly ignorant of the significance of the quality of the human factor to either the success or failure of the *laissez-faire* economic system (see Fusfeld, 2002, pp. 176-179). For this reason, they are unable to channel an adequate amount of the scarce FEET resources of the public into the enhancement of the quality of the human factor. And for as long as this level of blinding ignorance persists on the part of the free marketers, the social democrats will always return to the scene. And when they resurge with their sensually sweet lyrics and emotionally pleasing melodies and bags full of diverse forms of government assistance the members of the distraught and hopeless crowd will welcome them back with both arms to assume political leadership. They achieve this objective through the democratic process in the developed countries and military *coup d'état* in the developing nation states.

We must never ever forget that the ideology and worldview of the social democrats are powerful and makes a great deal of sense to the disposed, distressed, helplessly hopeless, the discriminated against, and those who have been ostracized for generations. As is most frequently presented and discussed with passion in the socialist literature, the benefits the social democrats allude to reflect the most important aspects and contributions of Marxism to the lives of the suffering people. Among these benefits, some of the best arguments made by social democratic scholars and political candidates include:

1. An excellent economic system must provide opportunities for everyone and ensure that people's dignity and human rights are respected, preserved, and protected.

2. The ideology of the social democrats define and present in passionately frustrated and angry manner the painful integrity crises and moral failures of the laissez-faire economic system.

3. Excellent philosophical expositions on the problems endemic to the *laissez-faire* economic system and how their presence ruins the quality of life for those discriminated against and shut out of the dream and hope for a better life.

4. The provision of an excellent philosophical as well as academic framework within which the problems of humanity, especially those of the suffering poor, can be dissected, analyzed, understood, and dealt with effectively and promptly.

5. The provision of powerfully convincing reasons to substantiate the desire to pursue massive political action through anger and dissent.

6. The reality that the philosophical and theoretical perspectives of the social democrat provide a glorious opportunity for the masses and political leaders and academicians to express their anger and frustrations against those deemed to be the oppressors. Through these, they offer hope and help to the people who experience oppression and rejection.

7. Everything in life is treated as a right rather than being either a privilege or something that one must have to exert

his or her own labour power to attain, sustain, and freely enjoy over the course of his or her own life.

These are great ideals (see discussions on these issues in Brue, 2000, pp. 168-185). They are most frequently appealing to most members of the general population. This is one reason why during hard economic times, anyone who runs a political campaign on this platform most often wins against counterparts who talk about hard work coupled with stringent measures that restrict the public budget and lower taxes.

Without being able to provide socialized methodologies and techniques through which the suffering and afflicted can attain and sustain these great ideals through the acts of the visible hand of government officials and the handouts they dole out, it is impossible to survive as an economic system. This is one of the most primary reasons why the *laissez-faire* economic system suffers severe setbacks and rejection during hard economic times. This is the case because people perceive and treat this inanimate economic system as the real source of their financial problems. Yet, unknown to these people, they are wrong in their thinking and beliefs about the free market economic system. To exist and/or survive, proponents of the *laissez-faire* economic system must find precise solutions to the pertinent and perennial problems faced by members of the disadvantaged classes.

Arguably, therefore, the philosophical and theoretical perspectives of the social democrats have a powerful ring of truth and hopefulness to them. They are the primary foundation for why the voices of the social democrats hold an excellent appeal to the suffering poor in the crowd. This is why it sometimes successfully sweeps certain long-term staunch free market enterprisers off their feet during moments of social upheavals and highly debilitating moments of economic distress. The empirical evidence that substantiates this conclusion is evident in the diverse messages of the electioneering campaigns for political leadership in the United Kingdom and the United States throughout the centuries. To a much larger degree, it is obviously evident in similar messages of those who vie for political leadership in the developing countries too.

Yet after having assumed the throne, the social democrats also fail miserably in fulfilling the tons of promises they make to their supporters. They hardly ever attain and sustain any long-term improvements in the people's quality of life despite the number of bills they succeed in passing into laws. They pride themselves in and boast of the number of bills they pass into laws. Sadly, though, their primary Achilles' heel and most debilitating source of failure is *severe human factor decay*. Viewed from this perspective, their own source of failure in dealing with the challenges that face the abject poor is identical to that of the free marketers! Arguably, therefore, both the free marketers and the social democrats agree that we have perennial problems that stall our efficiency in making the social institutions perform well. The sad part of the long-drawn saga between these two vehemently opposing groups of people is that none of their members actually knows for sure the precise root cause of the problems we face in the social institutions.

Until members of each of these groups come to the understanding that severe human factor decay is the primary root cause of our economic challenges and failing, they will continue to butt their heads relentlessly. Regardless of how fierce and prolonged these wars become, the problem of economic recession/depression will remain. The challenge of severe human factor decay will grow stronger and more deadly. As a natural outcome the perennial moments of the cycles of the flow and ebb of the activities of the proponents of the *laissez-faire* economic system as well as their activities of social democrats will become perennially entrenched. The undisputed long-term outcome will be the worsening nature of the human condition in the Global Village. Hopefully, members of these two non-compromising camps will learn the lesson so we can all sincerely work hand-in-hand toward the discovery of the long-term solution to our perennial problems of economic recessions and depressions.

The Six Dimensions of the Human Factor

There are six dimensions to the human factor. These include: *spiritual capital, moral capital, aesthetic capital, human capital, human abilities, and the human potential.* The description of each of these dimensions of the human factor is presented in Table 8.1.

Table 8.1: The Composition of the Human Factor

Components of the Human Factor	Definition
Spiritual Capital	The ability to connect to the universal principles of God (i.e., the connection to and with the natural laws of the universe)
Moral Capital	The ability to differentiate between right and wrong
Aesthetic Capital	The acumen to decipher and differentiate between what is beautiful and that which is ugly (i.e., the sense of beauty).
Human Capital	Knowledge and Skills
Human Abilities	Competences:—personal proficiencies in the application of knowledge, skills, and abilities (i.e., ableness, expertness, mastery, and expertise)
Human Potential	The yet to be tapped talents and dormant abilities (i.e., latent, unrealized, and dormant)

Source: The materials used to construct this table are from Adjibolosoo, S (1995). *The Human Factor in Developing Africa.* Westport, CT: Praeger.

Working together in concert, these dimensions of the

human factor, when well-developed enhance personal performance and productivity. Together, they ennoble the efficiency of the *laissez-faire* economic system. Arguably, it is a grievous mistake for members of any group of people to ignore the development of any of the six dimensions of the human factor (see Adjibolosoo, 2005, 1999, 1995a, b, and c). As argued in later chapters, the efficiency of the free market economic system depends on the degree to which every one of these aspects of the human factor is developed and effectively deployed.

The Role of Severe Human Factor Decay
Few people have understood the degree to which the quality of the human factor serves as the most critical variable that provides the solid foundation for the efficiency of the free market economic system. The quality of the human factor exerts tremendous impact on any person's effectiveness in the diverse marketplaces. With the definition of the human factor in mind and contrary to popularly held orthodox opinions about the sources of free market efficiency, no economic system, be it either capitalist or socialist or communist can attain and sustain its optimal performance in the presence of severe human factor decay.
In the words of Adjibolosoo (2009):
Severe human factor decay is a syndrome evident in a person's expression of lifestyle choices that are reflective of negative personality traits. It trumps the personal desire for virtuousness and promotes a lifestyle rooted in bad attitudes, behaviours, and actions. Severe human factor decay is the primary root cause of the human condition. Any act of social injustice is a perfect replica of the images of severe human factor decay...Severe human factor decay is a natural outflow of negative human factor. It is a serious hindrance to the establishment of harmony and peace. It is a staunch enemy to productivity growth. Its austerity paralyzes the engine—positive human factor—that makes the social institutions

function and remain functional over time. It stalls the wheels of the vehicles of family, government, schools, economy, law, and religion. It initiates and propels the uses and abuses of technological progress. It is the sole factor that lies at the heart of the practice of identity theft, sexual harassment, spousal/child abuse, and corruption in its diverse forms in any communities. Severe human factor decay damages the lives of citizens and denies them the ability to attain their human potential and sustain higher productivity levels. It renders these people unproductive. Their attitudes and behavioural practices are more destructive than constructive.

The human inability to deal precisely with severe human factor decay limits our capabilities and opportunities for overcoming the challenges to the effective functioning of our social institutions. Severe human factor decay is the foundational cause of social injustice in its diverse forms. As a devastating condition of the human mind and heart, it is a reflection of habitual practices that are bankrupt of principle-centeredness. It manifests itself in painfully destructive ways. When anyone's core of inner being is infested by the syndrome of severe human factor decay, he or she experiences total rottenness in the depths of his or her core of inner being. It underscores and promotes attitudes, behaviours, and actions that are reflective of selfishness and destructiveness.

Severe human factor decay results from a crippling high level of systemic corruption in a people's attitudes, behaviours, and actions. Severe human factor decay is the worst and most insidious roadblock to the efficiency of any economic system. Leaders of any governments or organizations that claim they can deal with severe human factor decay through the signing of bills into laws, implementing, and enforcing them have zero concept of what it is and the dangers it poses to society.

When the organization and administration of any government falls into the hands of certain morally and ethically bankrupted bureaucrats, business people, professionals, organizational leaders, and free market agents who too are corrupted in their avowed practices of business dealings and contractual arrangements in any marketplace, neither the strictest regulations nor most stringent punishment meted out to violators will heal a badly yoked *laissez-faire* economic system. Those who believe that they can erect massive welfare-based economic programs and pay for them by successfully imposing excessive tax burdens on the affluent citizens will fail in their bid to improve a people's quality of life. In addition, they cannot salvage any ailing economic system from its state of imminent recession and ultimate depression and ruin in the long-term.

There is sufficient reason for *the visible hand of government officials* to ascertain and sustain the efficiency of the free market economic system. The concept, *the visible hand of government officials* refers to the exercise of political authority in terms of engaging in acts of interference evident in the *laissez-faire* economic system with the purpose of dealing with inefficiencies evident in the free marketplace. However one of the greatest challenges we have faced throughout the centuries has been that any time we appeal to the visible hand of government officials, it has already been heavily tainted and corrupted even long before we solicit its intervention in the economy. Undeniably empirical evidence rules out certain government officials, business leaders, professional experts, social activists, and most members of civil society groups as the best cheerleaders for an effective economic recovery program.

Similarly, few of the most revered scholars of the discipline of economics possess any substantive notion as to what unleashes the forces that propel free market efficiency, ongoing economic growth, and sustained human-cantered development. For generations the lack of this vital knowledge has led to warped philosophical economic musing, thinking, and theorizing. The natural outcome of this lack of knowledge has produced faulty economic policies, ineffective plans, irrelevant   development   projects,   and   bankrupted socioeconomic programs.

The widespread ignorance regarding the primary factor that propels or militates against free market efficiency and economic progress poses enormous challenges to our ability to attain and sustain continuing economic growth and human-cantered socio-economic development. This high level of ignorance on the part of economists, government administrators, and a whole host of clueless politicians has also exacerbated the complex economic problems and policy failures that prevail in most nation states. These challenges create paralyzing waves of fear and hopelessness in people regarding what most political leaders and economists view as unmanageable tough economic downturns.

Our Failure

The failure to identify and deal with the true foundational cause (i.e., severe human factor decay) of economic recessions and/or depressions has dire consequences for long-term human welfare and advancement. The kinds of anxiety, restlessness, and frustrations experienced in most countries regarding recessions/depressions underscore the poverty of true knowledge and the lack of a deeper understanding as to how recessions and/or depressions happen and how to deal with them effectively. Traditionally global, national, and community leaders apply archaic theoretical solutions to the new problems created by old thinking with their unproductive results.

We haven't any deeper insights into the true underlying causes of the economic challenges we face. As a result we concentrate on the design and applications of solutions that are nothing more than reactionary ploys: ineffective quick-fixes and problem-accommodation measures.

The primary foundation of the long-term efficiency of the free market system is the high positive quality of the human factor. Any nations that are truly interested in transcending the challenges posed by recessions/depressions must engage in activities that lead to the honing of the positive qualities of the human factor. Undeniably, any improvements in the quality of the human factor will translate into sustained free market efficiency. Unless the positive qualities of the human factor are developed and effectively deployed, any attempts to deal with ensuing recession and/or depression will lead to suboptimal outcomes, further downturns, and massive loss of financial wealth.

One of the primary problems with orthodox economic theorizing and policy formulation today is the failure to recognize the significance of the quality of the human factor in economic modelling, policy formulation, project design, and program implementation (i.e., the 4Ps Portfolio). The performance of each aspect of the 4Ps Portfolio depends on the quality of the human factor of those in charge and their subordinates. The lack of understanding of the primary source of free market efficiency leads most *laissez-faire* economists and others who are its cheer leaders to err in their thinking about the triggers for economic slowdowns, recessions, and depressions. Almost every one of these scholars daily touts and celebrates free market policies as the sole solution to the diverse economic problems that beset us. Unfortunately, with the exception of Adam Smith (1776 and 1759) and a few others, not one of these modern economists has an idea about that which actually makes the free market economic system work efficiently.

Analyzing the previous, current, and future economic/business problems from the human factor perspective, we can argue that the only true source of any recessions—past, present, and future—and the diverse problems they create in the United States or elsewhere in the Global Village is *severe human factor decay*. Until our scarce FEET resources are channelled into more effective education programs aimed at improving the quality of the human factor, we will fail to revive sagging and stagnant market economies (see Adjibolosoo, 1996a and b).

That is, when we fail to produce the calibre of people required to deal with the economic problems we face, we fail. Those who implement and manage the social institutions of our time fail without having understood the importance of the quality of the human factor. Any *ad hoc* solution they apply serves only as short-term, stop-gap measures. They hardly ever work in the long-term. Since these solutions do not lead to any sustained improvements in the quality of the human factor in the long-term, we only successfully but temporarily postpone the more severe economic catastrophe.

In what follows in the remainder of this book, we will apply human factor analyses to sharpen our understanding of why we experience economic recessions/depressions and the failures we experience through the applications we make of quick-fixes and problem-accommodation measures.

9

Ebbs and Flows in the Laissez-Faire Economic System

One of the best ways to understand what a recession/depression is and how to deal with it effectively is to perceive the economy as if it were a massive building whose landed property is caught in the grasp of an expansive economic downturn or *the earthquake*. The landed property in question is the moral ground. It is critical to be aware that the foundational force that causes this shaking of the moral ground is *severe human factor decay*. That is, the critical force that causes the violent shaking of the building, the economy, is the morally decaying quality of the people's human factor. The landed property that is forcefully but irregularly shaking represents the shifting of the moral grounds. The force that shakes the landed property is severe human factor decay. The emergence of severe human factor decay is an outcome of people's failures to hone the positive qualities of their human factor.

The strength of the power of severe human factor decay is expressed daily in people's attitudes, behaviours, and actions as they interact with each other in infinitely diverse ways in the *laissez-faire* economic system. Examples of such interactions during which severe human factor decay plays out itself include the business of buying and selling, making contractual agreements, the offering of warrantees and guarantees, getting into and building relationships, the provision of diverse services, and any other economic activities like these. The shifting of the moral grounds as expressed in the existence of severe human factor decay is the primary trigger for any economic downturn. The amplitude and the degree of transition between the negative and positive aspects of the human factor determine the length and periodicity of the ebbs and flows inherent in the downturns of the *laissez-faire* economic system.

Dealing Effectively With Economic Recessions

With this delineation of the occurrence of economic downturns in the free market economic system in mind, the pertinent question then is: *How does one go about to minimize or stop the continual and violent shaking of the moral grounds on which the economic building has been established so it can be rescued from total deterioration, degradation, and ultimate collapse? For if the precise actions are not taken to deal with the force of the economic earthquake which is severe human factor decay, the magnitude of wealth losses will be traumatically devastating.*

To answer this question, we must perceive that it is impossible to prevent the established economic building from experiencing total devastation or some level of damage during the earthquake of the shifting moral grounds. If the foundation of the building had not been built according to the necessary moral principles to equip it to successful move in synchronicity with the rhythm of the economic earthquake, nothing else can be done successfully to prevent it from experiencing a total collapse will work.

A violently throbbing economic building is not all that easy to prop up or rescue if no one knows exactly the nature, power, and direction of the strength and force of the degradation of the moral grounds as revealed in severe human factor decay. Any economic building that has already been caught in the grasp of the irregular rhythms of the waves of the shifting of the moral grounds is not easy to prop up. Any attempts made in a rush to rescue it will not work if it has not been built to withstand the expressions of attitudes, behaviours, and actions rooted in the human factor decay. The expressions of treacherous attitudes, behaviours, and actions are initiated by the shifting of the moral grounds. Secondly, if the functioning of the *laissez-faire* economic system has not been built according to the moral principles that can sustain it during the violently throbbing of the moral grounds, the cause the economic earthquake, and if no one knows exactly the primary source of the exact force that propels the movements of the moral grounds, no one can save it from its ultimate demise.

However, if the *laissez-faire* economic system is constructed with a propelling blend of materials drawn from the moral principles that form and sustain its foundations, it will successfully dance rhythmically with the degree of severity of the economic earthquake. This outcome is an excellent reflection of the expressions of the positive human factor in action. When the economic earthquake subsides and its series of aftershocks are completed, the economic building will remain intact or suffer some minor structural damages! The amount of wealth loss will be minimal. These perspectives are reflective of the significance of the possession, understanding, and the ability to apply our knowledge of that force which causes an economic earthquake and the factors that sustain it.

The level of successes attained in dealing effectively with any economic earthquake is not a result of the number and strength of artificial props that are hurriedly put together by the visible hand of government officials during the moments of the economic earthquake. Neither will any haphazardly concocted economic recovery programs that are mounted as props to prevent any long-term damages. Instead, it is the result of long-term learning, understanding, and the ability to apply the knowledge of the causes of economic earthquakes and the nature of the economic building materials used and the requisite moral principles adhered to during the construction process. The failure to take advantage of this learning frequently spells great disaster for members of communities whose economic systems are built on treacherous and morally bad fault lines.

Distinguishing Recession and Depression

Similarly, economic recessions/depressions and how to deal with them effectively mimic the economic earthquake scenarios described above. The emergence of moments of an economic recession or depression is akin to that of any actual real life earthquake. Whether to categorize the nature of any economic downturn as a recession or depression depends on the intensity of the severity of the devastation it causes to life and property—the sum total of a people's wealth—during the period within which this event occurs. The extent to which any economic downturn destroys a people's wealth and the length of the time period it takes to dissipate are the key factors that determine whether to label any ebbing of the economy as a either recession or depression. Regardless of whether the economic problem on hand is a recession or depression, the primary causal factor is the degree of the severity of human factor decay.

In communities where the quality of the human factor is disproportionately negative an economic recession will linger on for as long as no appropriate actions are taken to restore the rotting core of the spiritual and moral foundations on which a virtuous economic program is based. Problem accommodation measures and quick-fix solutions may only temporarily postpone the final doomsday of any initiated economic downturn. Such quick-fixes and problem-accommodation measures emerge from actions taken by leaders of government officials at all levels. These measures are based on strict legal sanctions and the strength and effectiveness of their enforcement.

While a great deal of time is spent on the creation and implementation of these solutions, those who suffer from severe human factor decay engross themselves with their own faulty understanding of the new legal measures and how to transcend and benefit from them at the costly expense of others. The actions taken by the visible hand hardly ever attain the long-term intended objectives. The recession/depression becomes entrenched. It causes tremendous havoc by way of property loss and the devastation of a people's lives and wealth creation process.

Undeniably economic recessions/depressions are birthed when a people abandon the requirement that they live their lives according to the dictates of the moral principles of their own avowed standard. A people's set of moral principles provides the required guidance to succeed in everything they do. To abandon the Moral North and its prescriptions is to have already depleted the quality of the spiritual capital and moral capital (see details in Table 8.1 in Chapter 8). Sadly, when any people lose moral restraint, they deplete the quality of their spiritual capital and moral capital too. By depreciating the quality and de-accumulating the stock of these forms of vital capital, the economic earthquake is refuelled to throb and shake as violently as it is capable of and goes out of rhythm.

The quality of the human factor affects every sphere of life. Examples of certain aspects of life and human performance are listed in Table 9.1. In the first column is a listing of the social institutions and other aspects of human performance in organizations and systems. In the second column is the listing of specific spheres of individualized lives impacted by the quality of the human factor. Regardless of the moment of time under consideration the quality of human affects performance in every one of these areas of life. The economic earthquake in the form of a recession or depression wrecks a total havoc in communities where it occurs. In general, its destructiveness may either increase further or minimize the degree of the severity of human factor decay.

When an economic earthquake is triggered and becomes a true reality, those who desire to stop it and therefore place the economy back on the track of flow must first gain the precise knowledge and a deeper understanding of the quality of a people's human factor at that point in time. This knowledge must be appropriately channelled into actions aimed at subjugating the problem in the various spheres of life.

Table 9.1: The Human Factor Foundation of Action

The Quality of the Human Factor is always Prominent in:	
Organizations, Institutions, Systems, Practices, Ideologies, and Perspectives	*Personal Activities*
1. Politics and *Government* Operations 2. *Family*: Marriage, Divorce, and Child Raising 3. *Education*: Its Direction, Quality, and Reform 4. The Design and Enforcement of *the Law* 5. *Religion*: Spiritual Life and Clergy Performance 6. *Economics* and Business: Directions and Operations 7. Global Business Operations and Competitiveness 8. Business and Economic Activities in Countries 9. Institutional and Organizational Effectiveness 10. Ideological Perspectives and Effectiveness 11. Identifying and Meeting Human Needs 12. Demand for and Supply of Goods and Services 13. Human Attitudes, Behaviours, and Actions 14. Building Organizations and Strategic Relationships 15. Nature and Quality of Governance 16. Leadership and Managerial	1. Drug Addiction 2. Personal Health 3. The Provision of Any Services 4. Criminal Activities—Deviance 5. Lifestyle Choices 6. Bankruptcies and Failures 7. Personal Relationships 8. Contractual Arrangements 9. Honouring Promises and Words 10. The Pursuits of Self-Interests 11. Behavioural Inertia 12. Personal Professional Practices 13. Interpersonal Relationships 14. Individual Crises Response 15. The Nature of Cyber Activities 16. Individual Technology Use 17. Human Interactions 18. The Selection of Music/Art

Effectiveness
17. Conflict Resolution and Cooperation
18. Productivity Management and Growth
19. Decision Making and Team Effectiveness
20. Invention, Innovation, and Technological Progress
21. Nature and Quality of a People's Culture
22. Disaster Responses and Management
23. Athletic Performance and Competitiveness
24. Entertainment Industry in every Sphere
25. Promoting Human Rights and Freedom
26. Creating and Solving Environmental Problems
27. Professional Conduct and Competence
28. Human Dealings and Social Contracts
29. Financial Analyses and Fraudulence
30. Leadership and Management
31. Child Raising and Education
32. Educational Quality and Practices
33. Fundamentalism of any Kind
34. The Diverse Market Places
35. Financial Practices in Every Sphere of Life
36. Others

19. Acts of Sexual Harassment
20. Dealing with Limitations
21. Wealth Creation and fame
22. Dealing with Strangers (Others)
23. Spouses and Children
24. Treating others who Offend
25. Daily Frustrations
26. Losing Out to others
27. Speaking about others
28. Giving and Receiving
29. Personal Excellence
30. Individual Handiwork
31. Communications
32. Selected Reading Materials
33. Collegiality and Collaboration
34. Hygiene and Cleanliness
35. Alcoholism and Obesity
36. The Spoken and Written Words

The failure to accurately identify and understand the source of the recession/depression will lead to the fashioning and the application of problem accommodation measures and quick-fix solution sets. These are propelled by ignorance, fear, and the refusal to affirm the re-establishment of badly shaken moral grounds back to the original pristine form.

This reality is reflective of the nature of the initial attempts made to contain the problem of the BP oil spill in the Gulf of Mexico in April 2010. Until the true cause of this kind of oil spill was found and addressed, everything tried initially to solve the problem was a wasted effort. This has been the true reality throughout until some sort of a workable solution was found and effectively applied later than July 2010. Of course, the applications of trial and error methods do lead to good results some of the time. But when life is at stake, like those of Natasha and Humpty Dumpty, it is far better to be in possession of excellent knowledge of the true source of any problem rather than pursuing a solution that is based on trial-and-error attempts.

To know the true source of any problem is to have advanced about ninety percent toward breaking the back of the challenges it poses to a community of people. This brings great relief, peace, and hope to the problem solving process. The remaining ten percent of the problem-solving process is for the design, implementation, and the monitoring of the effectiveness of the solution.

These empirical observations regarding economic recessions/depressions are reflective of the quality of a people's human factor. They are great indicators of the successes and failures of those who design, implement, and run our educational enterprises and the nature of the curriculum they propose, pursue, and enforce. The gross failure of our educators to recognize the true significance of the quality of the human factor to a people's economic growth and human-cantered development is a painful travesty. In general it is this failure that emboldens political leaders to erect plans and policies that exacerbate rather than arrest the problem.

We must never erroneously assume that any recession/depression is a result of the inefficiencies we may observe in the functioning of the *laissez-faire* economic system. Instead, we must treat them as the true reflections of the degradation of the qualities of a people's spiritual capital and moral capital (see Table 8.1 in Chapter 8). They are undeniably reflective of the shifting of the moral grounds on which the economic building has been originally established. The recognition of this truth and the willingness to pursue educational programs aimed at strengthening the qualities of the spiritual capital and moral capital is the first critical step in the right direction. The second critical step is following through with the design and implementation of a human factor-based education program to improve the quality of the human factor in the long-term (see Adjibolosoo, 1996a and b). The long-term implications of these actions are economic rejuvenation and higher total factor productivity.

Externalities: When the Invisible Hand Fails

Another area where challenges emerge from in the laissez-faire economic system is referred to as externalities in economics. In what follows is a brief presentation on externalities and their true source. It is pointed out that as a serious economic problem that leads the invisible hand astray, we have been grossly unable to minimize it because the kinds of solutions we pursue to deal with this problem fail to address its precise root cause—severe human factor decay.

In traditional economic thinking, unhindered competitive markets are said to be efficient in what they do. Working freely through the price mechanism, competitive markets are said to provide proper incentives to producers for the purposes of efficient allocation of their available scarce FEET resources. The invisible hand is deemed to be the main force that guides producers and consumers to arrive at the point of optimal allocation their productive resources. When the conditions for the efficient functioning of the *laissez-faire* economic system exist, the invisible hand works unhindered. Under the conditions of freedom to operate, the invisible hand guides market participants in the *laissez-faire* economic system to arrive at *allocative efficiency*.

This result of allocative efficiency is reflective of the allocation of the available scarce FEET resources to the best alternative uses. What this means is that the invisible hand guides producers to manufacture and market exactly what consumers have effective demand for. Arguably, scarce FEET resources are never wasted on the production of goods and services nobody demands. Theoretically speaking, in the state of allocative efficiency, goods and services are said to have been produced using *the least costly methods, they are* sold to consumers at the best (lowest) equilibrium prices.

Yet as we have already discussed, in reality the equilibrium competitive price and the quantity exchanged in the free marketplace are determined through the interactions that occur between the forces of demand and supply. As is well known in economic analysis, while the consumer's demand curve is representative of his or her marginal private benefit (MPB), the supply curve reveals the marginal private cost (MPC) of the producer. Thus, when the invisible hand is left unhindered, the competitive price and equilibrium quantity exchanged is determined when the consumer's marginal private benefits are identical to the producer's marginal private costs. That is, in equilibrium in an efficiently functioning *laissez-faire* economic system, MPB = MPC.

Unfortunately, though, in cases where the invisible hand is led astray in the competitive marketplace the price mechanism fails to serve as an appropriate incentive. As a result, producers and consumers alike are led astray and do not arrive at the most efficient allocation of the available scarce FEET resources in the market place. This result in the free market economic system is what economists have referred to as a market failure. It is said to have been caused by factors external to the free market economic system. These external factors bring either positive or negative outcomes. Producer generated positive externalities that are not taken into account in the production process lead to under production of the commodity or service.

Contrariwise, the unaccounted for producer generated negative externalities lead to over production of the commodity or service. In general the challenges these externalities pose to society are the results of the failure to base the production process on social marginal benefits and marginal costs rather than private marginal benefits and costs. As is well known in economic analysis, market failure can occur when externalities emerge from monopolistic behaviour and the possession of asymmetric information as is the case in situations of moral hazard and adverse selection in insurance.

Generally defined, externalities happen when the attitudes, behaviours, and actions of economic agents either positively or negatively affect other third parties. These third party impacts are not necessarily taken into account when people engage in market transactions. That is, the impact of people's decisions on others (i.e., the third parties) is neither rewarded for the benefits they confer on others nor punished for the costs or damages they impose on others.

Positive externalities occur when the attitudes, behaviours, and actions of one party bring beneficial effects or some form of gains to others. An excellent example of positive externalities is the case of the symbiotic relationship between honey and apple producers. Though each of these farmers benefits tremendously from the other they never make any official payments to each other. As a result they produce less output of the commodities they produce (see Meade, J. 1952). In this example, as is usually the case, neither producer compensates the other for the benefits being freely enjoyed. Each producer ends failing to produce the optimal output level. In the event there are positive externalities the implication is that the social benefits are not equivalent to private benefits. As such, the socially optimal output level of production is not arrived at.

Negative externalities occur when the attitudes, behaviours, and actions of one party bring harmful effects to another party or group of individuals. Take, for example, the case of your roommate's smoking habits. If you are not a smoker, you are unfortunately subjected to second-hand smoke. Another example relates to a company that produces chemicals and during the process pollutes the drinking water of some villagers. In the situation of negative externalities, it is always the case that the marginal social cost (MSC) exceeds the marginal private cost (MPC). As a result the quantity of the commodity produced and placed on the market for sale is far bigger than the quantity required for the attainment of the socially optimal output. In the event this is the case the market is said to fail in that it overproduces the good. Other examples of negative externalities include pollution in its diverse forms as chemical, air, and environment. Others include diverse forms of congestion as evident in broadcasting, drivers on highways, and drilling in its diverse forms.

Arguably, externalities are mostly outcomes of severe human factor decay! Unfortunately, though, few economists make this link between the quality of the human factor and externalities. As a result, we continue to search for mathematical solutions to this real life problem. At best, we have concluded that negotiations as per *Coase's Theorem* and/or taxation are the best solutions for positive and negative externalities. Yet, since the problem of severe human factor is never addressed externalities never go away. *Coase's Theorem* recommends the assignment and enforcement of property rights to people. By so doing, people have the right to solve any problems they experience through peaceful negotiations.

10

Human Factor Foundation of Free Market Efficiency

To respond to the set of queries we must first gain a deeper understanding of what the true foundation of free market efficiency is. A thorough and critical study and analysis of the concepts of demand and supply reveal that most economists are unaware of the underlying forces of demand and supply. Due to this lack of knowledge and understanding, most of these scholars in this discipline talk about demand and supply forces as if their origin is from another planet or the blue skies!

This lack of knowledge and understanding on the part of these scholars is the primary origin of their misconceptions about the real determinants of demand and supply forces.

In orthodox economic theorizing the causal factors of demand and supply are attributed to considerations that are outside the quality of the human factor. Few economists or business managers, government leaders, and consumers know with certainty what the origin of demand and supply forces is.

Since a deeper level of analytic thinking from the human factor perspective in economic theorizing is non-existent in modern economic analyses, its vacuum produces misleading results.

Any serious economic modelling based on this kind of academic reasoning produces misleading conclusions, bad policy recommendations, faulty program design, and project implementation. These poor outcomes are the results of the unawareness of disciplinary academicians regarding the source of demand and supply forces. More serious scholars and students of economic analyses must transcend superficial thinking in economic theorizing, model building, and policy design. They must educate themselves to become more familiar with the real source of demand and supply forces. They must gain a deeper understanding of how interactions among people in the free market economic system determine and impact its operations. It is easy to discover whether people understand what the real determinants of demand and supply are. To do so, ask any economist or a non economist at random about what he or she perceives to be the actual factor that underscores the functioning of free market economic forces. When you hear any of these individuals suggest that the free market forces must be given more freedom to do what they do best, the additional question to pose to them is: *Where do market forces originate and what determines their nature, quality, intensity, and efficiency?* If any of these people can't tell you in an unequivocal manner that the primary factors that underlie the nature and strength of demand and supply forces are *attitudes, behaviours, and actions* propelled by the quality of the human factor, which is in turn rooted in either the adherence or disobedience to moral principles, they lack a good understanding of how free market economic forces work. In addition to this, they have neither an idea nor any clues about that which lays the foundation for the efficiency of the free market economic system.

For centuries economists of diverse persuasions have been oblivious of this knowledge. These are the economists who argue without being in possession of any concrete supporting empirical evidence that substantiates their conclusion that the free market economic system is efficient and the best there is among all other economic systems. More often than not, to most of these scholars, the effectiveness of the market economy is determined by the existence of efficient institutions, the assignment of property rights, the liberty to exercise one's labour power, the right for good education, the authorization to acquire and dispose of property, and all the other freedoms. Examples of these freedoms and/or rights include those of voting, information, speech, religion, movement, association, justice, peace, from fear, and from want. Unfortunately, though, these are all wrong answers to the question under investigation! They are wrong answers because most proponents of *laissez-faire* economic system do not understand well what makes these freedoms possible at all and how they are sustained.

Most people possess little understanding as to why free markets work efficiently. First, their pride roosts in the unsubstantiated belief that free markets just work. They are, unfortunately, clueless about why free markets work at all. Secondly, they maintain that individuals who act in free markets pursue rational decisions, un-coerced actions, and unhindered self-interests. Thirdly, they maintain that the free market economic system works well when property rights are clearly-defined, well-developed, assigned, and aggressively enforced. They, however, do not possess any inkling as to why these rights are well-defined, developed, assigned, and effectively enforced in some societies and not so well in others! By thinking in this manner most economists and free market enterprisers fail to highlight the degree to which the quality of the human factor underscores the validity and existence of each of these freedoms and opportunities in the free market economic system. This is because they are not aware of the relevance of the quality of the human factor to the existence of these great freedoms and opportunities in the countries that have them.

Primary Source of Demand and Supply

Viewed from the human factor perspective, we recognize demand and supply forces are unleashed by the nature and quality of *people's attitudes, behaviours, and actions*. Real life empirical evidence drawn from human relationships and interactions in the diverse free marketplaces reveals that underlying every human attitude, behaviour, and action is the quality of the human factor. Positive qualities of the human factor such as integrity, honesty, trust, accountability, and responsibility affect the functioning of the forces of demand and supply in a virtuously propelling direction. The presence of these qualities in any community tips the scale on the side of virtuous living. However, *negative* qualities such as greed, selfishness, unforgiving attitudes, hatred, deceitfulness, unfaithfulness, fraudulence, vindictiveness, and envy unleash and push demand and supply forces in directions that hinder sustained economic growth and human-cantered development. In this case, the human factor scale tips on the side of attitudes, behaviours, and actions that are non-principle-cantered.

While one person purchases a certain kind of product, another person may not buy such a product for numerous reasons. The quality of the human factor is the primary source of the mode and efficiency with which demand and supply forces function in the *laissez-faire* economic system. As any brilliant economist knows, a person's decision to engage in any buying behaviour is determined by both the strength of personal purchasing power and either the desire to exercise it or must possess the preference for the item. There is no effective demand for any commodity when either any of these factors is missing or both do not exist. Undeniably, a person's preference for any commodity or service is a reflection of the quality of his or her human factor.

In light of these empirical realities, a true understanding of how free market economic forces of demand and supply operate is incomplete without the personal awareness of the degree to which the quality of the human factor impacts the diverse consumer decisions in the free marketplace. People, propelled by their own attitudes, behaviours, and actions or those of others either push forward or hinder the efficiency with which free market forces function. It is people who give life to or impoverish the free market forces. The degree of effectiveness of the *laissez-faire* economic system rests powerfully on the foundation of the quality of the human factor.

Similarly, the constant flow of interactions among humans

determines what happens through market networks and operations. Free market forces emerging from the attitudes, behaviours, and actions of market agents are either moral or immoral depending on whether people who act in these markets are *virtuous* or *dishonest*. It is the strength of people's moral authority and character that serves as the exclusive foundation of the efficiency of the free market economic system. Undeniably, the *laissez-faire* economic system is propelled or paralyzed by the quality of the human factor.

Role of External Sources of Motivation
Let us continue on in this chapter with an undeniable truth from the human factor perspective. In the real world almost every person has come to believe that external sources of motivation such as monetary rewards lead to greater performance and higher personal productivity. Though nothing could be further away from this belief, it is also an excellent representation of the follies we accept as truth in terms of the precise sources of sustained levels of personal motivation. Sadly, though, we relentlessly pursue this belief in the *laissez-faire* economic system to our long-term undoing and detriment. For certain top notch orthodox economists want to force the rest of us to believe that market agents respond to financial incentives. As such, the economic argument is that once monetary incentives exist and free market agents are left on their own, they will pursue their own self-interests to the best of their abilities; and by so doing, produce the best outcomes for themselves and for the rest of society.

This belief is a blatant lie! In the presence of severe human factor decay, the free market forces are never able to attain their best results, even when the monetary incentives are excessively highly. If only we will learn that the quality of any individual's human factor is what drives him or her from the core of inner being, we will then be more successful in our quest for higher productivity and the quality of life it brings.

For when a person's core of inner being is filled with

spiritual capital and moral capital, he or she will perform most of the time at his or her best regardless of the nature and magnitude of externally-based rewards and/or punishments. Inner-directed people are more effective than those that are driven or guided by externally directed promptings. Free market agents who are inner-directed have what it takes to ensure the effectiveness of the *laissez-faire* economic system. It is in the absence of members of this calibre of people that the invisible hand is led astray. In the event this is the case, free market forces (i.e., human agents) falter as a result of severe human factor decay.

Contrariwise, the moral ineptitude of players in the free market economic system destroys its long-term efficiency. The attitudes, behaviours, and actions of human beings who possess the positive qualities of the human factor enhance free market efficiency through the orderly and principle-cantered expressions of their attitudes, behaviours, and actions. Unfortunately, though, the attitudes, behaviours, and actions of those who suffer from severe human factor decay lead *the Smithian Invisible Hand* astray. Worst of all, by misleading the invisible hand of government officials, the activities of the visible hand are initiated, signed into laws, implemented, and enforced.

These actions produce the corrupted interventions and practices of the agents of the visible hand of government officials. The free market forces are hindered in the wealth creation process when they are replaced by corrupted human actions. These individuals' sentiments of degeneracy are inherent in their core of inner being. The nature of the expression of free market forces is immoral when humans who interact with each other are salacious. Whether markets are moral or prurient depends on the quality of the human factor of people who participate in market activities in the *laissez-faire* economic system. In general, therefore, while principle-cantered attitudes, behaviours, and actions ennoble free market efficiency, unprincipled practices engaged in by unprincipled market agents destroy it in the long-term.

The ongoing interactions between the forces of virtue and licentiousness determine the efficiency of free markets in the *laissez faire* economic system. The *Invisible Hand* performs well when virtuous habitual practices that emerge from positive human factor, the sole foundation of free markets, win. On the other hand, the *Invisible Hand* is led astray when the forces of human depravity, the substructure of the negative human factor or severe human factor decay win over those of virtue. Herein lays the main source of the quality of market efficiency.

Quality of the Human Factor and Free Market Efficiency

Long-term free market efficiency requires the availability of the highest possible quality of the invaluable *spiritual capital* as well as *moral capital* in individual actors. While a person's spiritual capital connects to the universal principles, the moral capital determines the ability to differentiate between right and wrong. Of a great significance to the efficiency of free market forces is the positive quality of the components of the human factor. When each of these components declines precipitously in its quality, the efficiency of the key players in free markets diminishes. In free markets the reality of human depravity is revealed in the deterioration and expression of attitudes, behaviours, and actions in business dealings and other kinds of interactions at the marketplace. The decay in the quality of spiritual capital and moral capital militates against sustained economic growth and enduring human-cantered development. These problems spawn lack of accountability, irresponsibility, and low productivity.

The free market economic system is an inanimate institutional arrangement. It is primarily a human creation to be used as a tool to deal with the scarcity problem. As such, the primary task of its human agents is to inform and create diverse interactions among themselves as demanders and suppliers of goods and services. Working together in concert, these human agents determine and enforce the quality of the goods and services offered at the marketplace. In the common event where these human agents are corrupt, the efficiency of the free market economic system is corrupted. In and of itself the free market system neither possesses any inherent requisite power nor authority outside what human attitudes, behaviours, and actions equip it with. People use the quality of their human factor to establish customary practices that fuel and power their Codes of ethical behaviour within the free market economic structure. They agree to voluntarily live by or are forced to comply with these institutional arrangements to foster efficiency in the functioning of the free market economic system.

These conventions are enforced to induce the players to practice their trades according to the stipulated Codes of ethical conduct. People are expected to merchandise their products according to the dictates of their own avowed universal moral principles and ethical standards. People's considerations of and respect for these establishments in their pursuit of economic activities enhance the wealth creation process in any community or nation. When gross and pervasive violations take place in the *laissez-faire* economic system, the whole economic system breaks down. The invisible hand of government officials is decommissioned. The visible hand rises and takes its place. Yet as noted earlier, this replacement rarely works well because the Visible Hand of government officials is severely tainted!

Those who violate any of these underlying moral principles of virtue by acting against the stipulations of the virtuous conventions of the free market economic system are punished when discovered. Manufacturers who offer poor quality products and services are punished when their customers vote with their feet in the long-term—after having become aware of fraudulence on the part of the producer. Their loss of market shares spells their ultimate doom. When these violators evade detection and don't get caught and punished instantly to deter others from continuing on in a similar manner, their perverse actions, in a combined manner, ruin the efficiency of all the players in the free market economic system in the long-term. The current recession which began to reveal its preliminary signs in 2007 in most developed countries, especially in the United States and other advanced countries is an example of this reality. To voluntarily abide by the diverse institutional arrangements designed to foster free market economic efficiency is to enable the reality of its performance optimality. The nature of people's performance in free market economies is an excellent reflection of the quality of the human factor.

The necessity of having to impose more regulations to force people to respect the dictates of existing sanctions aimed at promoting efficiency in the free market economic system is an admission of the degree of the nature of the decay inherent in the people's quality of the human factor. Stated differently, the speed of the proliferation of the law and legal sanctions in their numerous forms illustrates the depth of severe human factor decay in any society. It is impossible for individual players in an inanimate system or social institution to function honestly on their own volition without having developed positive human factor. The animating input from the positive quality of any person's human factor impacts his or her performance in free markets. If the human input into the functioning of the free market economic system, is devitalizing, those who participate in these markets are unable to produce at the desired level of efficiency. Succinctly stated, severe human factor decay destroys the efficiency of free market forces by either slowing it down or thwarting completely the national wealth-creation process. Such interventions exert tremendous transactions costs on the effectiveness of market agents.

Relevance of the Impartial Spectator
The diligent reading and re-reading of Adam Smith's

(1759) book, *The Theory of Moral Sentiments*, reveals that the manner in which attitudes, behaviours, and actions are expressed exerts a tremendous impact on the efficiency of human agents in the free market economic system. The strength of the authority of personal sympathy for others and the respect for and obedience to the prescriptions and proscriptions of the *Impartial Spectator* act as the sole gatekeepers of the degree to which moral principles are adhered to. The kinds of emotional feelings, desires, and sentiments people express in social relationships in market structures are first and foremost reflections of the quality of the human factor.

Secondly, the quality of the human factor reveals the effectiveness of the authority and power of personal sympathy and reverence for the rules of engagement established by the *Impartial Spectator*. These rules are the dictates of the universal principles. No humans have any control over the validity and enforcement of these principles. These enforce themselves without fail—regardless of the length of time it may take them to pronounce the just and final verdict. Whether or not people express or suppress any moral sentiments is determined by the quality of their own human factor.

Any individuals who express their self-interests in subordination to the dictates of the universal principles ennoble the potency of human action in the free market economic system. The positive human factor qualities of people who dabble in the free market economy create long-term efficiency. Contrariwise, the pursuit of degenerated personal self-interests (i.e., interests that morph into the personal engagement in acts of greed and selfishness) deadens positive free market outcomes.

Severe human factor decay is the primary cause of any forms of economic instability, recession, and depression. When the strength of the desire to engage in acts of personal selfishness trumps human consanguinity, people's actions in the free market economic system become corrupted. The strength of malfeasance of the members of diverse groups of people weakens the authoritative voice and the virtuous guiding principles of the *Impartial Spectator*. This level of depravity in the quality of the human factor leads those who suffer from it to design and pursue devious patronage schemes. These concocted machinations hurt innocent individuals.

The primary objective of those who design such schemes is to illegally and secretly profit at the expense of others. Whatever happens to those who unknowingly accept these schemes and get hurt thereby is of no concern to the despicably unscrupulous designers. The long-term implications of these acts of human degeneracy in free markets lead to the total collapse of the efficient functioning of the *laissez-faire* economic system. The severity of this disintegration depends on the strength of the turpitude of those who suffer from the throes of severe human factor decay. The only long-term solution to the hindrance to human efficiency in the free market economic system is the development of the positive qualities of the human factor.

It is only when personal acts of benevolence and respect for the dictates of the universal principles reign supreme in people's minds and hearts do waves of selflessness and self-control remain obedient to the guiding voice of bridled conscience. Those individuals whose positive human factor qualities are more developed are able to internally police their own actions regarding everything they do in the free market economic system. When the unyielding voice of a principle-cantered conscience trumps the feelings of personal selfishness, people's prudence in exercising sound judgment, justice, and the unwillingness to dabble in acts of fraudulence win over the lure of personal affluence acquisition and the desire to engage in acts of wrongdoing. Economic and business environments filled with this calibre of people encourage efficient performance in the free market economic system. Contrariwise, this reality is not the case for those who suffer from severe human factor decay. It is undeniable that the pursuit of self-interested attitudes, behaviours, and actions that crave social approval in contradistinction with the dictates of universal principles of virtuousness endangers the efficiency of people serving in free markets.

Implications of Warped Notions

One of the greatest challenges participants in free market economies face is the warped notion that the creation and accumulation of personal wealth is desirable regardless of the means by which it is acquired. This belief and the kinds of moral sentiments it arouses decimate the efficiency of human interactions in the free market economic system. It destroys the potency and long-term survivability of the free market economy. Human attitudes, behaviours, and actions are only in consonance with the principles of moral virtue when the quality of people's human factor is more positive than negative. The core of inner being is equipped with live conscience based on universal principles. The quality of personal moral condition is *sine qua non* to consistency in engagement in virtuous attitudes, behaviours, and actions in the free market economy. In the long-term self-interested pursuits that lack moral conditioning hurt the effectiveness of human agents operating in the free market economy.

The primary source of the strength or weakness of human operations in free markets is the quality of the human factor. Analogously, the optimization of human efficiency in free markets depends on the quality of the human factor as well. No human beings can claim perfection in the quality of their own human factor. Neither can any individual perfectly express his or her attitudes, behaviours, and actions. Therefore, the combined interactions among people in free markets can only achieve a certain level of maximum efficiency. The greatest possible efficiency attainable in the free market system is that which is supported by the degree to which the expressions of the positive human factor qualities trump those of the negative.

Similarly, when the combined negative human factor

qualities of all players in the market overwhelm those of the positive, the proficiency levels of the players in free markets revert to their barest minimum. This reality is what triggers and sustains recessions as well as severe depressions for as long as they are not detected and corrected in good time. While the presence of the negative quality of the human factor in the core of inner being of a select few may not cause and sustain severe recessions or depressions, that of a large number of individuals operating in the free market economy will. When the expressions of the positive qualities of the human factor trump those of the negative human factor, performance in the free market economic system is enhanced.

Morality of Economic Systems

As inanimate economic systems, neither capitalism nor socialism is inherently immoral. Only intelligent and wise people are aware that the effectiveness of any of these economic systems depends on the quality of the human factor. People who are rather habitually immoral will destroy the efficiency of the free market economic forces as well as those of socialism and/or communism. Any improvements being called for regarding any of these economic systems must first deal with the quality of the human factor of the participants. When higher levels of efficiency are desired in the social institutions, employees, leaders, managers, and those served must advance in the quality of their human factor.

This is why the human factor theorist maintains that while the expression of a single individual's attitudes, behaviours, and actions may not significantly impact economic activities in the *laissez-faire* economic system that of a larger number of people will. The only exception to this rule is the case in which the individual is the leader with the full authority and power on his side or has monopoly power in an industry. Every severe recession or depression we have experienced in human history or will witness in the future is solely attributable to no other sources than that of severe human factor decay.

Effective and efficient human action in the free market system requires that habitual practices be in line with the dictates of the universal principles. By being subject to the immutable laws of nature that have their own way over time, human action will yield optimum productivity. Regardless of the inclinations and intentionality of a few people who disobey these precepts, free market efficiency will be attained. It is only when most market agents intentionally violate these principles due to severe human factor decay that market inefficiency and failure occur.

Place of the Law

When humans adhere to the dictates of moral principles there is no need to create a jungle of laws that are forever conflicting. By living by the dictates of universal precepts, there is no need for any intrusion into people's lives via legal manipulations. The need for costly interventions through the actions of the visible hand of government officials would be minimized in the long-term. It can only be done away with when everyone morphs into a perfect human being! Unfortunately, as noted earlier, this outcome is impossible among spiritually ignorant and morally bankrupted human beings. The *laissez-faire* economic system is at its best performances during periods when people willingly and intentionally adhere to universal spiritual principles and moral virtues. Sustained economic growth and efficiency of humans require loyalty to the dictates of the universal principles.

If only intellectuals drawn to the discipline of economics will transition from the point of mere intelligence to that of wisdom, it is possible that we can work hand-in-hand to discover the human factor foundation of the successes and failures of free market participants.

By so doing we become better-positioned to make wise contributions toward our quest to find long-term solutions to the challenges we face in making the social institutions work efficiently. This is a humongous task requiring all hands to be on deck if our desire is to succeed in minimizing the intensity of the painful seasonal as well as the long-term cyclical challenges we face in our free economic market transactions and their implications for economic growth and sustained human-cantered development. The sources of the answers to the problems we face remain dormant in the quality of our individual and combined human factor.

Goal of the Visible Hand of Government Officials

The theoretical analyses we make reveal excellent quantitative prowess and academic brilliance on our part. They, however, ignore the most significant variable, *the quality of the human factor of business leaders as well as that of their clients* and the visible hand of government officials. In the financial markets it is the quality of the human factor that determines the true health and ability of any bankers to lead their banks to experience profitability and long-term survival. In the presence of severe human factor decay, it is impossible for managers, employees, and consultants of any banks to survive regardless of the amount of available capital or the total amount of bailout money it receives from government. As the American International Group's (AIG) experience has revealed in no uncertain terms, funds are frequently misapplied, mismanaged, and/or misappropriated in legally intelligent ways in the short-term! In the long-term, such unprincipled human actions force the whole financial system to either collapse or be placed on a precarious life support by the visible hands of government officials.

In light of this conclusion, it is undeniable that if the goal of the Visible Hand (i.e., government officials) is to ensure the long-term profitability and survival of banks and other business organizations, their effort must be directed primarily at improving the quality of the human factor. Their 4Ps Portfolios must be aimed at forging improvements in the quality of the human factor. Without this any achievements made regarding the survival of banks, the real estate market, the stock market, and other business organizations will be short-lived. This is because these gains will be chipped away by those who suffer from the syndrome of severe human factor decay. Quick-fix solutions neither work well nor remain relevant for long in the free market economic system. They are built on a shaky intellectual foundation. They easily crumble when additional quick-fix solutions and problem-accommodating structures are subsequently laid upon them. We must avoid their use to concentrate our scarce FEET resources on the 4Ps Portfolios that have the capability to enhance the economic condition in the long-term. If possible at all, we must use them sparingly.

11

Developing the Positive Qualities of the Human Factor

There are many views regarding the meaning and constituents of economic prosperity; however, sustained economic growth and human-cantered development must focus on honing the quality of the human factor. This action ensures improved performance and the general wellbeing of every community member. Working together in concert those who design and manage programs aimed at economic progress must ensure liberty. By so doing, their leadership and managerial practices will give birth to hope and guarantee personal fulfilment for all.

These ideals can only be attained and sustained when there is authentic respect for and obedience to the dictates of the universal principles of supreme truths among community members. People must promote love and respect for their neighbours among all community members. Yet the practice of these may be impossible without the personal growth in and commitment to engage in attitudinal and behavioural practices that exude kindness, compassion, and forgiveness. To create an epoch of ongoing economic growth to sustain the nation building effort, citizens must channel sufficient expenditure of their scarce FEET resources into programs to improve the quality of the human factor.

Source of the Solution Set

To prepare the next generation of leaders for the workplace, it imperative to provide graduate as well as undergraduate students with excellent business education that will lead them to pursue and attain results beyond mere bottom line considerations that are based on self-centeredness that is devoid of avowed moral principles and ethical standards. This kind of education is not necessarily about the acquisition of academic knowledge in various areas of business. Instead, it is about the creation of the appropriate educational environment within which each student is exposed to a program of activities that promotes growth in personal character.

While doing so, students will be exposed to all functional areas of economic activities and business ventures. They will also be guided to understand better to significance of the quality of the human factor to either successes or failures in economic activities and business organizations. The human factor qualities required for succeed in each functional area of economic activities and the business practices are highlighted and discussed in this chapter as well as subsequent ones. The ongoing exposure of students to reading materials must lead to the development of the six dimensions of the human factor as listed in Table 8.1. It is about the positive transformation in their personality characteristics as these students voluntarily pursue business education programs that focus on human factor development.

The intentionality with which this course is designed and taught is geared toward a diversity of activities and efforts that educate principle-cantered students. Everything we do must be viewed as a means to the ultimate end, principle-cantered education. We must know that whether we either succeed or fail in our mission of educating students in principle-centeredness, we will be graduation and sending them out to the economic and business world. Upon having been educated on the foundation of principle-centeredness, each student, after graduation, will continue to build a strong ethical foundational knowledge base for sound economic activities, principle-cantered business decision making, moral character formation, and the ability to engage in sound ethical choices and practices. This education program will enhance the moral and ethical balance of graduates from the diverse educational institutions.

The primary source of the solution set does not only rest in assisting people to hone their positive human factor but also requires an understanding of that which forms the true foundation for the humanness of every one of us. This truth is evident in the deeper insights Robert Maynard Hutchins expressed a few decades ago (January 17, 1899–May 17, 1977). It seems to me that at the time when he expressed these sentiments and insights, those who heard him neither understood the depth and gravity of his excellent perspective nor cared in any meaningful way. Today, though we sincerely need his insights, we too are neither uninterested nor care at all about their relevance to the efficiency of our social institutions—especially economics. Yet, he was truly aware of the deepest core of the problems we experience in our inability to make the social institutions, of which economics is one, to function efficiently and remain functional over time.

Hutchins is right when he observes that:

Society is to be improved, not by forcing a program of social reform down its throat, through the schools or otherwise but by the improvement of the individuals who compose it. As Plato said, "Governments reflect human nature. States are not made out of stone or wood, but out of the character of their citizens; these turn the scale and draw everything after them. The individual is the heart of society."...To talk about making men [women] better we must have some idea of what men [women] are because if we have none, we can have no idea of what is good or bad for them...A sound philosophy in general suggests that men [women] are rational, moral, and spiritual beings and that the improvement of men [women] means the fullest development of their rational, moral, and spiritual powers. All men [women] have these powers, and all men [women] should develop them to the fullest extent.

Undeniably, *a healthy normal human being* is indeed, *rational*, *moral*, and *spiritual*. From these we can add that such an individual is emotional too. Arguably, the items that constitute this list is infinite and unknown to us in its entirety.

Yet, over the centuries, we have refused to acknowledge and nurse the spiritual dimension of our being without any convincing empirical evidence to back our claims and attitudes. Even in cases where we acknowledge the moral dimension of our beingness, most of us prefer to live by our own situational and/or relativistic ethic. Most of us have concluded and believe that every one of us must be guided by his or her personal truths and ethics. Viewed in this light, let your own truths and ethics be yours and grant that mine remain solely mine without any questions asked. If, however, we have any disagreements and conflicts to settle you must without any questions yield to the applications of my ethics to settle every dispute we may have.

To reject my standards is to be a bigot. You are both a racist and hard core self-cantered person. You hate and disrespect others who are different. By so doing, we have muddied the moral waters so badly that we just do not have any sense of that which is right and wrong any more. The quality of our moral capital is weak and continuously declining in worth.

Piggybacking on this reality is our own combined confusion about that which constitutes beauty. And since we cannot even resolve this one, we have hurriedly concluded that when you are not sure about anything, you must just go ahead and do that which feels good and right to you. After having accepted and continually lived our lives by this dictum for centuries, we are now at a place where we cannot make the social institutions we have created as tools to deal effectively with our perennial problems to work as efficiently as we desire. As existing empirical evidence and historical data have revealed and confirmed we are swimming up against and drowning in the vicious currents of our own problems. Though the right solutions chase after and cry at us loudly and incessantly, we are too busy looking through the clogged lenses of our intellectual microscopes and telescopes at locations where we will never ever discover the true solutions we sincerely must have. We diligently and passionately zoom in and zoom out through the lenses of these tools and other kinds of the technologies we fashion. But much of this is to no avail. What a pity!

Thinking much more deeply about how we may go about to discover a set of solutions that will work for us, Hutchins (1953) notes further that: "Unless we can figure out what education is and what a university is and unless we can build up a tradition in this country [and in every human community] that supports these conceptions, education and the universities will always be at the mercy of those of those who honestly or for political purposes seek to make them the protagonists of their views" (Quoted in Hoff, 2009, pp. 203-217). Hutchins is right when he notes that "The object of the educational system, taken as a whole, is not to produce hands for industry or to teach the young how to make a living. It is to produce responsible citizens" This perspective of Hutchins is aimed at the pre-emption of the vocationalist critique of contemporary higher education.

Sadly, though, we are stuck in educational quagmires that have little usefulness in terms of preparing us to find our way out of the thick, deep, and expansive woods of intellectualism, doubts, and confusion. Today, we do exactly that which Hutchins believes will never lead us to our intended and desired destination. We do education to train the mind to reason in only a certain way. We fail to position the trained mind to also pursue growth in the spiritual and moral dimensions of life. Sadly, our education programs for centuries have led us too far away from our hope of finding workable answers we so desperately seek.

To deny the relevance of the quality of the human factor and fail to hone it is to have injected poisonous venom into the blood stream of every community member. Members of any communities who suffer from this traumatic experience will also be victims to that which annihilated the dinosaurs. From one ancient generation to another, *ad infinitum*, we continue to repeat the educational follies of the members of our preceding generations.

Members of any communities who ignore the significance of the quality of the human factor to the effectiveness of their social institutions do so to their own peril. The empirical evidence to this effect is overwhelming. Throughout the centuries members of the preceding generations thought they could do anything they desired to the total neglect of effective educational programs to hone the positive qualities of the human factor. None of us needs to be conversant in rocket science to perceive the folly in the thoughts of some of our great grandparents.

Unfortunately we too continue to follow blindly in the footsteps of those who preceded us. Yet members of these preceding generations made the messes we have inherited and suffer from. Albert Einstein is right in his perspective about the challenges we face and the insanity evident in our solution.

Lee Kuan Yew, a former Prime Minister of Singapore, speaks powerfully about the significance of the quality of the human factor in nation building. His perspective holds true for institution as well as community and nation building. The positive qualities of the human factor are critical to our effectiveness and any successes we attain in the functioning of the social institutions we employ. Speaking to this issue upon his critical review of *the Goh Report on Singaporean National Education Plan*, Lee Kuan Yew observes:

The first subject concerns good citizenship and nationhood. What kind of man or woman does a child grow up to be after 10-12 years of schooling? Is he a worthy citizen, guided by decent moral precepts? Have his teachers and principals set him good examples? Imparting knowledge to pass examinations, and later to do a job, these are important. However, the litmus test of a good education is whether it nurtures good citizens who can live, work, contend and co-operate in a civilized way. Is he loyal and patriotic? Is he, when the need arises, a good soldier, ready to defend his country? Is he filial, respectful to elders, law-abiding, humane, and responsible? Does he take care of his wife and children, and his parents? Is he a good neighbour and a trustworthy friend? Is he tolerant of Singaporeans of different races and religions? Is he clean, neat, punctual, and well mannered?

It is impossible to make any institution work without the availability of quality people. In the presence of severe human factor decay few people who manage the social institutions will achieve their intended objectives.

Adding his voice to the significant role people play in the social institutions, Schumpeter (1934) observes that:

People are the actors through whom strategy unfolds, as a result of which firms succeed or fail...People act, among other things, as owners, as entrepreneurs, as sources of skills and expertise, as collaborators, as participants in network and learning activities, as agents of their own carriers.... People as entrepreneurs are credited with special qualities such as strengths in judgment (Casson, 1982), a "will to conquer" (Schumpeter, 1934) or a "need for achievement" (McClelland, 1961), through which they succeed in founding new firms....Economic renewal depends then on the rise to leadership of "New Men [and Women].

Regardless of the importance of the new computer technology, the relentless channelling of scarce resources into its development and the mechanical training of men and women to operate them is creating benefits as well as phenomenal opportunity costs for humanity. Yet few people acknowledge and address these costs. The perennial focus on technological development, scientific research, space exploration, and legal initiatives leads to the diversion of our attention as well as scarce financial, effort, energy, and time (FEET) resources away from the development of the human factor. The more advanced, intelligent, and sophisticated our technologies and knowledge become the further we move away from the total development of the positive human factor. This phenomenon derails the train of our quest and zaps away the ability to find the path to a life of tranquillity, harmoniously peaceful co-existence, and long-lasting satisfaction.

The quality of the human factor matters a great deal in ensuring free market efficiency. Existing empirical evidence has proven time and time again that the true foundation of the effectiveness of agents in the free market economic system is the blending of the positive and negative qualities of the human factor. For this blend to yield the expected positive results, it must be in the direction of virtuousness. This result will increase and sustain the wealth of nations. In the absence of this blend, problems increase in magnitude and jeopardize the virtuous cycle of productivity growth and sustained human-cantered development.

The glorious attainments of the agents of the *laissez-faire* economic system are not the result of the efforts of any social institutions at all. As noted earlier, institutions as well as organizations and systems that humans create for problem solving are inanimate. They neither perform nor possess any life of their own. Their effectiveness is solely determined by the quality of the human factor of those who implement, manage, lead, and evaluate their effectiveness. It is the quality of each of these people's human factor that determines the efficiency of every social institution. These people too play in the free market economic system. In the absence of quality people in the marketplace gross inefficiency reigns in the *laissez-faire* economic system. Both the invisible hand and visible hand of the government officials are led astray simultaneously. Neither of these hands can lead nor support any meaningful change or enhanced productivity of social institutions.

Worst of all, once the visible hand of government officials steps in, the invisible hand is most frequently put out of commission. It is most frequently not permitted to function as effectively as it possibly can. Yet, undeniably, the visible hand of government officials steps in when the invisible hand has abandoned the spiritual and moral foundations of the efficiency of the *laissez-faire* economic system.

The Essential Input for Free Market Efficiency

In view of the foregoing presentation the quality of the human factor is the most essential input required for the effective performance of free market economic system. The avid pursuit of principle-cantered self-interested attitudes, behaviours, and action opens the floodgates to increased wealth creation activities in the free market economic system (see details in Figure 3.1 in Chapter 3). Improvements in the positive quality of the human factor lead to decline in attitudinal, behavioural practices, and actions that are inimical to the efficiency of the *laissez-faire* economic system.

Roche (1987, p. xii) notes correctly that:

We are misled by our perspective. In seeing the heroic as too large for ourselves, we have been deceived and cheated by some seemingly innovative but unbalanced philosophies that see the human purpose as far too small. These anti-heroic philosophies, of which we have much to say...have been woven of scientific errors and prideful cravings...In sum, they constitute a sweeping denial of value and purpose to human life, setting us adrift in existence without meaning or hope...Destroying civilized life.

The result of the orthodox practice of ignoring the quality of the human factor in economic theorizing is that emerging economic theories, regardless of how fancifully mathematical and academically intelligent their authors may be, hardly ever lead us to the desired long-term solutions. In the long-term, the economic plans, policies, projects, and programs (the 4Ps Portfolios) they birth experience few successes in the short-term. These gains are most frequently washed away and community members are ferried back to square one—their original point of commencement—only to painfully start it all over again in the same manner! The theories and the 4Ps Portfolios these intellectual practices engender are frequently demolished by real life economic problems that face us from time to time. The prevailing empirical evidence in this regard is overwhelmingly damaging. These realities, however, underscore the empirical observation that the positive quality of the human factor is the sole foundation and medium of all economic progress and the efficiency of free market players.

The spiritual capital (i.e., the ability to connect to the ordained principles of the universe and moral capital (i.e., the ability to distinguish between right and wrong) are critically invaluable to sustained economic growth, social progress, and technological advancement. However, the applications of technology, innovation, and human welfare, and all forms of productive capital are currently being ignored or neglected (see Table 8.1 in Chapter 8). If, in fact, we don't reverse the trend of decay in the quality of our spiritual capital and moral capital, our civilization has no brighter future than what it is today. Our hope in the expected salvation from technological genius will lead us only to a painful dead end! I hope we will be readily willing and intentional about turning the human ship around long before it hits the imminent monstrously destructive iceberg!

That Which We Must Do and Avoid

Any groups of people who desire to build humane communities with veritable economic progress must avoid the total depreciation of the quality of their spiritual capital and moral capital. A people who are busily destroying their spiritual capital and moral capital will evince perennial economic stagnation, recession, and depression over the long term. Recent economic problems in the world economy are excellent examples of the implications of severe human factor decay for the performance of the social institutions.

The social institutions such as the family, government, schools, economy, religion, and the law require people who possess a better blend of both positive and negative qualities of the human factor to lead and manage them. Since the family is the main building block of any society, its destruction implies the annihilation of the effectiveness of the social institutions.

Yet to succeed we must be readily willing or learn to embrace the winds of change and turn our attention to the relevance and development of spiritual capital and moral capital. Our continuing experience of severe human factor decay will corrupt further the quality of our human factor. By so doing the fuel that powers the engine of our free market economic system will become diluted and rendered powerless. The cogs of the engine of the free market economic system will be filled with diverse hindrances that emerge from severe human factor decay. The reality of these problems propels the emergence of severe economic problems.

Throughout human history members of any community who experienced steady economic progress and excellent quality of life paid greater attention to the honing of the spiritual capital and moral capital. The failure to recognize the actual importance of both spiritual capital and moral capital in recent years in the United States of America and other developed nation states has led people to abandon their development. The custodians of schools, colleges, universities, and other institutions of learning have tended to solely focus on investment in human capital which is only a miniscule component of the human factor (see Table 8.1 in Chapter 8). The significance of the quality of the human factor to economic development and advancement in any nation state is the primary source propellant, and the methodical progression of advancement in diverse spheres of human life.

Our Education Reform Program

If we sincerely desire to turn *the seriously lost human ship* around and prevent it from premature destruction, we must pause momentarily now and rethink our existing education programs by taking a more critical and thorough look at their vision and mission statements. If we engage in this exercise with great intentionality and patience, we will without any doubts recognize that the kind of education program that will get us to *our desired destination is the one which transforms knowledge into wisdom through understanding.* This education program is what I refer to as *transformational development education.*

By transformational development education I imply the kind of education that provides a propelling academic environment within which the types of intellectual, spiritual, and moral activities pursued facilitate learning to equip the learners with knowledge, skills, and abilities to apply to problem solving. The learner is assisted to make use of what is taught and learned as well as honing the positive human factor qualities required to be patriotic citizens and honest and compassionate leaders. The primary object of everything done in this environment is to equip those who participate to develop the full dimensions of their human factor [see http://www.transcendingexcellence.com/TDE.html].

There is hope that we can succeed at breaking the back of the problems we face as we work to make our social institutions to function and remain functional over time. The greatest challenge, though, is whether or not we are truly willing to work hand-in-hand to take this journey. Regardless of what we decide to do, it is important we *ALWAYS* remember that the effectiveness we experience in the functioning of any of the social institutions is a direct outcome of the quality of our individual as well as the combined human factor.

12

Conclusions and Recommendations for Public Policy

When any people lose sight of the universal Moral North their spiritual qualities wane. A natural outflow of this reality is that their desire to express moral strength in daily lifestyle choices also declines precipitously. One of the most traumatic natural outflows of this reality is that the efficiency with which economic agents function in the *laissez-faire* economic system diminishes. Until the Moral North is re-established and economic/business activities are carried out in line with its dictates (i.e., prescriptions and proscriptions), every frantic action taken by the visible hand of government officials and other regulators through legal restrictions will never ever solve the problems being faced. Think a little deeper so you don't misunderstand this point.

There is room for the visible hand of government officials in ascertaining the efficiency of the free market economic system. Yet, one of the greatest challenges we have faced throughout the centuries has been that any time we appeal to the visible hand of government officials, it is already heavily tainted and corrupt even before we solicit its intervention in the economy. The numerous practices that confirm this reality include the following:

1. The Failure of Regulatory Enforcement.
2. There exists a cozy relationship between regulators and those they are charged to regulate and oversee so they do the right thing. This reality promotes and sustains the practice of the unspoken *quid quo pro* relationship between regulators and the regulated.
3. Parliamentary Acts and/or Laws are used as mere rubber stamps.

4. The general population is acutely ignorant and lacks the knowledge and sophistication required to monitor the diverse human agents of the visible hand.
5. Most frequently, the attitudinal and behavioural practices government officials who are morally tainted in their thoughts and actions engage in daily is never driven by principle-cantered self-interest pursuits. These greedy and deceptive government officials are also cold and calculated frauds. They do not have the moral authority and spiritual strength and insights it takes to make the effectiveness of any social institutions improve.

Undeniably, this overwhelming empirical evidence rules out certain government officials as the best monitors for any economic recovery programs anywhere in the whole world. Arguably, therefore, the performance of the *laissez-faire* economic system depends solely on the strength of the spiritual and moral qualities of a people's human factor.

Contrary to popularly held orthodox opinions about the source of the efficiency of the free market economic system, no economic system can attain and sustain its performance optimality in the presence of severe human factor decay. When government leadership falls into the hands of unwise and corrupted bureaucrats/leaders and at the same time free market agents are morally rotten to the core neither regulations nor stringent punishments will free the badly yoked *laissez-faire* economic system. Those who erect massive welfare economic structures and excessive tax burdens on certain citizens in free market economies will fail in the long-term.

We must never be fooled to think that we can both problem-accommodate and quick-fix our way through any recession/depression. We've done nothing to date about the core of the problem—severe human factor decay. By doing whatever it takes to strengthen the quality of spiritual capital and moral capital, we will improve our chances of putting the economy back on track again. The truth is that the combined puissance in these areas of our *beingness* will buttress the muscles of our moral strength and resolve to succeed at economic theorizing, policy making, plan formulation, project design, and program implementation May we never continue to gloss over this truth regarding how to make the economy work again for us.

In general the thoughts assembled and published in books provide powerful explanations for and solutions to the global recession/depression; previous, present, and subsequent ones too. National leaders who are interested in designing and implementing effective long-term solutions to the economic problems will do well to gain a better understanding of the significance of the quality of the human factor to sustained human-cantered economic development and ongoing growth.

It is obvious that without the right calibre of people devoted to the job for which they have been hired, not much will be achieved in terms of productivity growth, enhanced quality of life, and community harmony. This is why human factor decay is destructive to plans of conflict resolution, peacemaking, sustained economic growth, and human-cantered development. The failure to develop all the six dimensions of the human factor leads to the perennial decay in the social institutions. We continue to experience serious problems in the functioning of our social institutions due to severe human factor decay. There exist pervasively high levels of corruption and inefficiency among people in performing their leadership functions in every social institution.

When those in charge of running the social institutions fail in carrying out their duties, they're unable to decipher the true source of the problem as being severe human factor decay. In our combined ignorance we blame the inanimate social institutions, humanly-created systems, and organizations for having failed. We become blinded by our own ignorance and self-satisfied selves that we cannot acknowledge the degree to which we have depreciated the quality of our human factor.

Our degree of ignorance is often so wide, long, high, and deep that we are unable to recognize that we have created these institutions and their problems! We fail to perceive that these institutions are only as good and effective as we are in running them and solving the problems. Since these institutions, modern technology, and the 4Ps Portfolios we create are inanimate, any kind of life they have is what we give to them. They are only as good and efficient as we are in the core of our inner being. Since we create them, there is no way they can ever be any better than we make them. The failure on our part to comprehend this truth reflects why we are unable to solve the problems we have faced throughout the centuries. Undeniably, therefore, the failure of any of the 4Ps Portfolios, institutions, businesses, and organizations is human failure!

In this book the chapters together take to task the nature of the economic challenges being currently faced all over the world. The traditional explanations given to the causes of any recession and/or depression are rejected. Using human factor theory presented in this book and the discussions brought to bear on the theme of interest to us poignantly expressed the significance of human factor decay to economic recessions and depressions. It is concluded that until the quality of the human factor is improved it is impossible to minimize the frequency and intensity of economic recessions and depressions in any country. The contents of this book expose the diverse misconceptions regarding orthodox economic philosophical thinking, theorizing, and their attendant policy implications for free market efficiency.

It has been argued further in this book that to hone the quality of the human factor is to equip free market forces with quality people to pursue, attain, and sustain optimal economic outcomes of the wealth creation process. Undeniably, when a people lose sight of the significance of the quality of the human factor, the efficiency of their free market economic system declines. One of the most traumatic natural outflows of this reality is that the efficiency with which economic agents function in the *laissez-faire* economic system diminishes. Until the positive qualities of the human factor are re-established and economic/business activities carried out in line with the dictates of *natural liberty* and *laissez-faire* economic principles, every frantic action taken by government officials and/or other regulatory agents will not solve the problems on hand.

Conclusion

A people must do everything possible to avoid the reality of being fooled into thinking that they can engage in the practice of problem-accommodation and the applications of quick-fix solutions to transcend their prevailing economic problems. Sadly, government administrators, business leaders, and highly revered economists have done nothing to date about the core problem—*severe human factor decay*. It is important to know that by doing whatever it takes to improve the quality of the human factor we will enhance our chances of putting the economy back on track. The undeniable truth is that the attained puissance in the positive qualities of the human factor will buttress the muscles of our resolve to succeed at economic theorizing, policy making, plan formulation, project design, and program implementation. By way of recommendation, any people who desire to deal effectively with economic recessions, depressions, and any other socio-economic problems must begin with efficient education programs aimed at honing the positive qualities of the human factor (see Adjibolosoo, 2005).

As long as people continue to focus on dealing with symptoms rather than the actual root cause of prevailing problems, they will never achieve any form of lasting peace, tranquillity, happiness, and progress. Any people who desire to achieve these goals must acquire positive human factor without which their society and every social institution will crumble.

References

References

Adjibolosoo, S. (ed.) 1996a. *Human Factor Engineering and the Political Economy of African Development.* Westport, CT: Praeger.

Adjibolosoo, S. (ed.) 1998b. *International Perspectives on the Human Factor in Economic Development.* Westport, CT.: Praeger.

Adjibolosoo, S. 1993. "The Human Factor in Development." *The Scandinavian Journal of Development Alternatives,* XII (4): 139-149.

Adjibolosoo, S. 1994. "The Human Factor and the Failure of Development Planning and Economic Policy in Africa." In F. Ezeala-Harrison and S. Adjibolosoo, eds. *Perspectives on Economic Development in Africa.* Westport, CT.: Praeger.

Adjibolosoo, S. 1995a. The Human Factor in Developing Africa. Westport, C: Praeger Publishers.

Adjibolosoo, S. 1995a. *The Human Factor in Developing Africa.* Westport, CT.: Praeger.

Adjibolosoo, S. 1995c. "Achieving Optimal Quality and Productivity: The Passions." In D. J. Sumanth, J. A., Edosomwan, R., Poupart, and C. G. Thor, eds. *Productivity and Quality Management Frontiers-V.* Norcross, Georgia: Industrial engineering Management Press.

Adjibolosoo, S. 1996b. "A Guide to Understanding the Fundamental Principles of Human Factor Theory." *Review of Human Factor Studies,* 2 (1): 1- 26 [The full text is posted on the web site of the International Institute for Human Factor Development (IIHFD). The web site address is: www.twu.ca/iihfd.

Adjibolosoo, S. 1998a. *Global Development the Human Factor Way.* Westport, CT.: Praeger.

Adjibolosoo, S. 1999. *Rethinking Development Theory and*

Policy: A Human Factor Critique. Westport, CT.: Praeger.

Adjibolosoo, S. 2005. *The Human Factor in Leadership Effectiveness*. Oklahoma City: Tate Publishing.

Adjibolosoo, S. 2009. "The Human Condition and Plight: Sinking Deeper into and Digging Ourselves Out of the Miry Quicksand of Social Injustice." A paper presented at the Round Table—Oxford University, UK, March 22nd-27th 2009. The preparation and presentation of this paper at the Oxford Round Table have been financially supported by the Alumni Research Grant and the Faculty Professional Development Fund—Point Loma Nazarene University).

Adjibolosoo, S. ed. 1995b. *The Significance of the Human Factor in African Economic Development*. Westport, CT.: Praeger.

Blumberg, P. 1989. *The Predatory Society: Deceptions in the American Marketplace*. New York: Oxford University Press.

Brue, S. L. 2000. *The Evolution of Economic Thought*. New York: The Dryden Press.

Commons, J. R. 1989. *Institutional Economics: Its Place in Political Economy* (Volume 1). Piscataway, New Jersey: Transaction Publishers.

Commons, J. R. 1998. *John R. Commons's Investigational Economics*, Volume Archival Supplement (Research in the History of Economic Thought and Methodology). Greenwich CT: JAI Press

Commons, J. R. 2006. *Legal Foundations of Capitalism*. Clark, New Jersey: The Law book Exchange, Ltd.

Croce, B. 1941. *History as the Story of Liberty*. New York: W. W. Norton & Co.

Cypher, J. M. and Dietz, J. L. 1997. *The Process of Economic Development*. New York: Routledge.

De Vries, J. 1976. *The Economy of Europe in and Age of Crisis, 1600-1750*. Cambridge: Cambridge University Press.

Filler, L. 1939. *Crusaders for American Liberalism*. New York:

Harcourt, Brace, & Co.

Fox, S. I. 1987. *Human Physiology.* Dubuque, Iowa: Wm. C. Brown Publishers.

Friedman, M. 1953. *Essays in Positive Economics.* Chicago: University of Chicago Press.

Friedman, M. and Friedman, R. 1980. *Free to Choose: A Personal Statement.* New York: Harcourt Brace Jovanovich.

Hazlitt, H. 1988. *Economics in One Lesson: The Shortest and Surest Way to Understand Basic Economics.* Auburn, Alabama: Ludwig Von Mises Institute.

Hill, M. and Kwan Fee, L. 1995. *The Politics of Nation Building and Citizenship in Singapore.* New York: Routledge.

Hobhouse, L. T. 1911. *Liberalism.* New York: Henry Holt & Co.

Hobson, J. A. 1909. *The Crisis of Liberalism.* New York: P. S. King & Son.

Hoff, P. S. 2009. "Hutchin's University of Utopia: Institutional Independence, Academic Freedom, and Radical Restructuring." *Innovative Higher Education,* 34 (4th October): 203-217.

Hollander, J. H. 1925. *Economic Liberalism.* New York: Abingdon Press.

Hoover, H. C. 1934. *The Challenge to Liberty.* New York: Charles Scribner's Sons.

Hudson, M. 2000. "The Use and Abuse of Mathematical Economics." *Journal of Economic Studies,* 27: 292-315.

Hudson, M. 2009. Trade, Development and Foreign Debt. Hobart, Australia: ISLET.

Kasliwal, P. 1995. *Development Economics.* Cincinnati, Ohio: South-Western College Publishing.

Keynes, J. M. 1971. *The Collected Writings of John Maynard Keynes—Volume VI.* London: Macmillan.

King, , J. E. 1988. *Economic Exiles.* New York: St. Martin's Press

Kohlberg, L. 1958. "The Development of Modes of Thinking and Choices in Years 10 to 16". *Ph. D. Dissertation, University of Chicago.*

Kohlberg, L. 1971. *From Is to Ought: How to Commit the Naturalistic Fallacy and Get Away with It in the Study of Moral Development.* New York: Academic Press.

Kohlberg, L. 1981. *Essays on Moral Development, Vol. I: The Philosophy of Moral Development.* San Francisco, CA: Harper & Row.

Kohlberg, L., Levine, C., and Hewer, A. 1983. *Moral stages : A Current Formulation and a Response to Critics.* Basel, NY: Karger.

Krugman, P. 2009. "How Did Economists Get It so Wrong?" New York Times of September 2, 2009. http://www.nytimes.com/2009/09/06/magazine/06Economic-t.html?r=1.

Kuhn, T. S. 1962. *The Structure of Scientific Revolutions.* Chicago: University of Chicago Press.

Laski, H. J. 1936. The Rise of Liberalism: The Philosophy of a Business Civilization. New York: Harper & Brothers.

Marx, K. 1992. *Capital: Volume 1: A Critique of Political Economy.* New York: Penguin Classics.

Marx, K. 1993. *Capital: A Critique of Political Economy, Vol. 3.* New York: Penguin Classics.

Marx, K. 2009. *Capital Volume 2: A Critique of Political Economy.* Bel Air, CA: General Books LLC.

Marx, K. 2010. *The Communist Manifesto.* Scotts Valley, CA: CreateSpace.

Maslow, A. 1943. "A Theory of Human Motivation." *Psychological Review*, 50(4): 370-96.

Maslow, A. 1954. *Motivation and Personality.* New York: Harper and Row Publishers.

Meade, J. 1952. *Economic Journal,* 62 (March): 54-67.

Mill, J. S. 1947. *On Liberty.* New York: Appleton-Century-Crofts (Also published by Little Brown & Co., Boston, 1921).

Opie and P. Opie 1951. *The Oxford Dictionary of Nursery Rhymes* (Oxford: Oxford University Press (2nd edition, 1997).

Piaget, J. 1932. *The Moral Judgment of the Child.* London: Kegan Paul, Trench, Trubner and Company.

Poulson, B. W. 1994. *Economic Development: Private and Public Choice.* New York: West Publishing Company.

Robertson, J. M. 1925. *The Meaning of Liberalism.* London: Methuen.

Roche, G. 1987. *A World Without Heroes: The Modern Tragedy.* Hillsdale, Michigan: Hillsdale Press.

Roche, G. 1987. *A World Without Heroes: The Modern Tragedy.* Hillsdale, Michigan: Hillsdale Press.

Rosenberg, N. 1979. "Adam Smith and *Laissez Faire*-Revisited." In G. P. O'Driscoll, ed. *Adam Smith and Modern Political Economy: Bicentennial Essays on the Wealth of Nations.* Ames: Iowa State University Press.

Ruggiero, G. 1927. *The History of European Liberalism.* London: Oxford University Press.

Samuelson, P. 1939. "The Gains from International Trade." *Canadian Journal of Economics and Political Science,* Volume 5: 205.

Schumpeter, J. A. 1934. *The Theory of Economic Development.* Cambridge: Harvard University Press.

Screpanti, E. and Zamagni, S. 1993. *An Outline of the History of Economic Thought.* New York: Oxford University Press.

Skinner, C. R. 1937. *Liberalism Faces the Future.* New York: The Macmillan Company.

Smith, A. 1909. *An Inquiry into the Nature and Causes of the Wealth of Nations.* New York, P. F. Collier & Sons (Originally published in 1776).

Smith, A. 2009. *The Theory of Moral Sentiments.* Indianapolis, IN.: Liberty Fund Inc. (December 17, 2009). (Originally published in 1759).

Soule, G. 1937. *The Future of Liberty.* New York: The Macmillan Company.

Spender, S. 1937. *Forward from Liberalism.* New York: Random House.

Todaro, M. P. *Economic Development.* 1997. New York: Addison-Wesley Publishing Company.

Veblen, T. 2008. *The Theory of the Leisure Class.* Rockville, MD: Arc Manor.

Veblen, T. 2010. *The Theory of Business Enterprise.* Charleston, SC: Nabu Press.

Vickery, W. S. 1964. *Microstatics* New York: Harcourt, Brace, and Wold.

Von Mises, L. 1949. *Human Action: A Treatise on Economics.* New Haven: Yale University Press.

Wasserman, L. 1944. *Modern Political Philosophies and what they Mean.* Philadelphia: The Blakiston Company.

Index

Index